#recharge

The Ultimate EV Travel Guide for Europe

"Acting more sustainably should not stop with driving an electric car, but it is a good start!"

Mr & Mrs T on Tour

#recharge

The Ultimate EV Travel Guide for Europe

teNeues

THE JOURNEY TO A MORE SUSTAINABLE FUTURE

Our life-changing adventure as "Mr & Mrs T on Tour" began in 2015, when we were looking to buy a new car. Who would have thought at the time that choosing a Tesla might lead to a two-year road trip around the world … and to the publication of this book?

Since we love to travel—and like staying at beautiful hotels—we took our Tesla Model S on wonderful weekend trips, totally emission free. Charging en route was as easy as making use of the overnight destination chargers at the hotels with charging stations. Not every hotel we visited was able to support guests traveling by electric car and even if they had charging facilities, some failed to deliver one of our key criteria—an environment in which we could sustainably re-charge our own batteries. But that is exactly the point: literally and figuratively filling up with positive energy, whether you are traveling for two weeks or just over the weekend! Our favorite hotels scored with their empathetic philosophy, their clear positioning, and the authenticity of their mission. They always ensured high quality and excellent service, as well as fresh energy.

We wanted to discover new destinations where we could recharge our car's batteries as well as our own, and share the experience with others. What began as a weekend trip soon became a life-changing concept. The idea for #recharge, our first EV Travel Guide, was born. However, it quickly became clear to us that we did not want to make a recommendation without first having been there and experienced a destination ourselves. So how could it work? We reflected on this question until we visited a Tesla customer event in Fremont, California, in June 2017. There, Tesla chief designer Franz von Holzhausen gave us the decisive impetus. We realized that sometimes you just have to leave your own comfort zone to achieve something special.

We asked ourselves in the hotel that night, "Could we possibly imagine leading a life on the road and letting go of everything else?" It didn't take long to make our decision. Only a few months later, we quit our jobs, and cancelled the lease on our home in Switzerland, put all our belongings into storage, and set out on our electric adventure in April 2018. Having bid farewell to our family and friends, and to the members of the local Tesla Owners Club, we set off, accompanied by a Tesla Film Crew who documented the beginning of our journey. "The weekend getaway that never ends" had begun.

But that was just the beginning of the story, because traveling changes you, and it does so in a lasting way. Being on the move using an electric-powered car is not only fun—it has also opened up a path for us to a more sustainable future. From our point of view, it's therefore true to say: "Acting more sustainably should not stop with driving an electric car, but it is a good start!"

We have made it our aim to experience the world in a more sustainable fashion, to learn from other people and cultures along the way, to experiment with new ways of living, and to become more self-aware. We want to help accelerate the global transition to sustainable energy, which is not necessarily about being perfect, but rather about rethinking your actions, recognizing better options, and, above all, acting on them. It is often the little things that lead to the biggest changes, and every single person can make a difference with their own contribution.

This combination of an illustrated book and travel guide is intended to inspire you and allow us to share our insights with others. It is an invitation to try something new—to just head off and discover some of the special places that have enchanted and captivated us on our journey. Many of the hotels we are presenting not only provided outstanding accommodations and service, but also strove to take their guests back to nature in a stylish way. They provide their guests with an opportunity to replenish lost energy,

which encourages positivity. Respecting human beings, nature, and the environment is a central part of each hotels' concept, and a strong basis for sustainability. These hotels pay attention to detail and have the greatest respect for the natural resources they use. They are places that tell a story worth listening to. The hosts and their team are passionate about their mission, innovative in their approach, support the local community, and treat every guest as a family friend. And they don't just offer a bed for the night—a visit to the perfect hotel is a life-affirming, memorable, rejuvenating experience.

We hope this book is only the beginning of your journey to a more sustainable future. We wish you a lot of fun and positive energy along the way.

Mr & Mrs T on Tour,
Ralf Schwesinger & Nicole Wanner

CONTENTS

Switzerland & Liechtenstein

Germany

Austria

Scandinavia

Traveling by Electric Car 210

PORTUGAL

CASA MOCHO BRANCO
Loulé, Portugal

As you enter the Casa Mocho Branco, a mere fifteen minutes inland from the Algarve you will discover a little oasis of hospitality behind the imposing, large white gate.

hotel info:

Casa Mocho Branco
Estr. Jogo de
Gilvrasino
P-8100-337 Loulé-
Parragil
Tel.: +351 289 419540
Mail:
genietenindealgarve@
gmail.com
Web: www.
genietenindealgarve.
com

charging facilities:

1 Tesla DeC (Tesla only)

Casa Mocho Branco's website name translates from Dutch as "enjoying the Algarve"—and their guests' pleasure and relaxation are precisely what the Netherlands-born owners, Brandina and Dik focus on at their small bed and breakfast. The beautifully appointed guesthouse sits on a slight foothill, providing a magical view over the turquoise infinity pool, the Algarve coastline, and even the deep-blue sea beyond. And the incredibly beautiful garden is a similar feast for the senses. Guests are accommodated either in the small private villa featuring a delightful terrace and pergola, or in one of the three rooms in the main building. All the rooms

Mr T: "As pleasant as this hotel is, make sure you venture out to explore the surroundings. Some of the Algarve's most beautiful bays are found right here."

are tastefully furnished to perfection, and the atmosphere is warm and friendly, just like a family home. You meet the hosts and other guests over breakfast, where Brandina serves homemade cakes and vitamin-rich fruit platters, and in the lush garden or by the pool, over a cup of coffee in the lounge, at dinner, or on the spacious balcony overlooking the pool. Here Dik operates the barbecue, and ensures all his guests are in a perfect holiday mood.

AROUND LOULÉ
Portugal

Steep rockfaces and magical bays on Portugal's dream coast

A beach vacation in Portugal immediately conjures up the Algarve. The coast here is lined by 65–164ft (20–50m) high yellow or reddish limestone and sandstone rocks, interrupted by delightful coves revealing picture book beaches with fine, golden sand.

Loulé
(approx. 6¼ miles/10km)

It is only a short drive to the traditional market town of Loulé, whose administrative district also includes Parragil, where the Casa Mocho Branco is located. The historic center of Loulé is typically Portuguese, with picturesque lanes, the Moorish Loulé Castle, a fascinating local history museum, and several small churches. The Mercado Municipal de Loulé, which sells locally made food, textiles, and gifts, was built in 2007, and its architecture was also inspired by Moorish styles. The market hall is home to a large farmers' market every Saturday morning. Yet, the panoramic views of the Algarve from Loulé can be enjoyed every day—simply walk up the hill from the old town to the church of Nossa Senhora da Piedade.

Vilamoura
(approx. 9¼ miles/15km)

The fantastic location, where the typical reddish cliffs of the Algarve coast briefly give way to a few miles of flat, sandy beach, was no doubt one of the reasons why Vilamoura was established near the small resort of Quarteira in the mid-1960s. In addition to numerous upscale and luxury beachside hotels, Vilamoura is also home to Portugal's largest yacht harbor, where over 1,000 boats are moored all year round. Cafés, restaurants,

Mrs T: "Lying in the styled bathtub in the detached small villa, you can look up and marvel at the starry sky."

bars, boutiques, and the casino are all clustered around the picture-postcard marina. This is also a great destination for golfers; they can take their pick from five different courses situated a short distance from the beach, while bathers, kite-surfers, and beach walkers enjoy life down below by the sea.

to celebrate

One of Portugal's most colorful carnival parades is the Concurso Carnavalesco, inspired by the parades in Rio de Janeiro. On the long carnival weekend, it proceeds through the Avenida José da Costa Mealha in Loulé, watched by thousands of spectators.

Loulé Carneval
First weekend of March

PARAISO ESCONDIDO

São Teotónio, Portugal

The Paraiso Escondido, or "hidden paradise," boutique hotel is located in the wild and sparsely populated Alentejo in southwestern Portugal, providing its guests with a peaceful escape in breathtaking countryside.

hotel info:

Paraiso Escondido
Caixa Postal 5550-A
P-7630-568 Casa Nova
da Cruz (São Teotónio)
Tel.: +351 91 2470206
Mail: info@
paraisoescondido.pt
Web: www.
paraisoescondido.pt

charging facilities:

1 Tesla DeC (Tesla only)
1 Tesla DeC (all EVs)

The countryside inland from the Atlantic coast, with its open landscapes and clear starry skies reminded Mozambique born Berny Serrão of her homeland, which was why she created Paraiso Escondido Hotel with her partner, Glenn Cullen, as a homage to her "lost Africa." The flat building with columned porch sits on top of a mountain like a luxury safari lodge, providing fabulous views over the pool and down into the valley. The hosts have painstakingly styled the eight rooms and suites in keeping with the motto, "We want to sell an experience, not a room," accentuating the decor with unique pieces acquired on their travels in Africa and Asia. For guests

Mr T: "Berny and Glenn share their travel experiences, in addition to their unique artifacts from Africa and Asia, with the hotel guests."

wishing more privacy, two secluded bungalows on stilts appear to float amidst lush surrounds between the mountain and the sky! And if you fancy a little company, simply head back to the large common area in the main building for a chat. This is where the organic breakfast is served every morning, as well as dinner in the evening made with fresh, home-grown ingredients—the hosts place great emphasis on sustainability and quality.

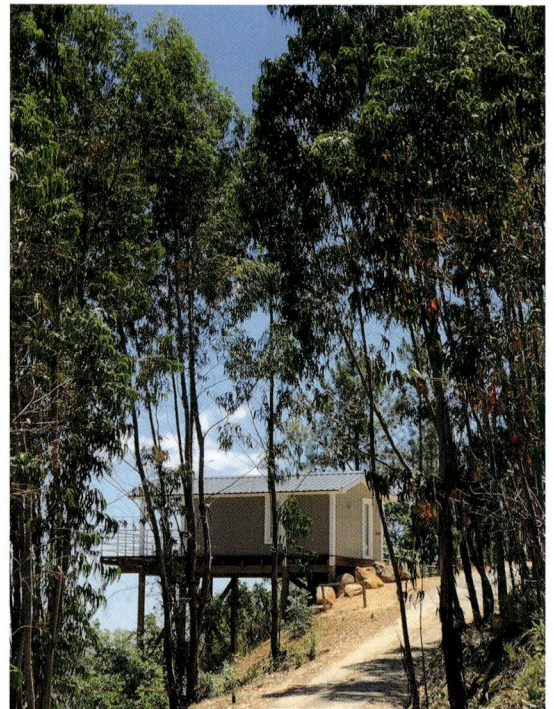

AROUND SÃO TEOTÓNIO
Portugal

Quiet tranquility and wild beauty at the end of Europe

Discover beautiful, sparsely populated coastal landscapes with craggy rocks, sandy coves, forests, dunes, bogs, and salt marshes in Portugal's—and mainland Europe's—extreme southwest. Barren countryside here alternates with areas of dense vegetation.

**Parque Natural do Sudoeste
Alentejano e Costa Vicentina
(approx. 9½ miles/15km)**

One of Portugal's most beautiful nature parks, the South West Alentejo and Vicentine Coast Natural Park, founded in 1988, extends along the coastline from São Torpes in the north to Burgau beyond the Algarve's most southwesterly point at Cape St. Vicent. The middle section of this virginal coastal landscape is only a fifteen-minute drive from the hotel. Ospreys, otters, and white storks live here; unique to this area, the storks here nest in the cliffs. The region also encompasses the Rio Mira Valley, which reaches as far inland as Odemira. A network of 280 miles (450km) of hiking tracks in the Rota Vicentina unlock the wonders of the nature park, with the four 12½ mile (20km) stretches of the *Trilho dos Pescadores* (the Fishermen's Trail), which follow the coastline, considered to be the most spectacular.

Sines (approx. 43 miles/70km)

The small coastal town of Sines is about a one-hour scenic ride north. The Romans valued Sines as a maritime base, and today it is home to both a small fishing port and to a large industrial and container port. Rising up beyond the colorful moored fishing boats is the picturesque old town, where a statue of Vasco da Gama (c. 1469 to 1529, below) stands

Mrs T: "It's the most remote places in nature that open your eyes—and your heart. That gives a real boost of energy."

at its entrance, gazing out to the Atlantic. The town's most famous son, he discovered the sea route to India around the Cape of Good Hope (1497–99) and later became Viceroy of India. He is believed to have been born in the fortress that, similar to the Fort do Revelim, served to defend Sines from pirates.

to eat

The Porto das Barcas restaurant, located right on the Atlantic Ocean, is less than 25 miles (40km) from Vila Nova de Milfontes. As you would expect, freshly caught fish and seafood are served in (almost) every conceivable variation.

Porto das Barcas
Estrada do Canal S/N,
P-7645-000 Vila Nova de Milfontes

↑ The hotel is located in the middle of the countryside and surrounded by dense forest. Its rooms feature floor-to-ceiling windows, allowing plenty of light and superb views of the rich, green countryside.

PENA PARK HOTEL

Ribeira de Pena, Portugal

The Pena Park Hotel is situated in northern Portugal's green hills and forests. Surrounded by an abundance of flora and fauna, it offers its guests rest and relaxation as well as a great base for action-packed activities in the area.

hotel info:

Pena Park Hotel
Rua do Complexo
Turístico de Lamelas, 2
P-4870-110 Ribeira
de Pena
Tel.: +351 259 100880
Mail: info@
penaparkhotel.pt
Web: www.
penaparkhotel.pt

charging facilities:

4 Tesla DeC (all EVs)
10 Tesla SuC (Tesla only)

The new four-star Pena Park Hotel is distinguished by its unique location. Set in the lush natural environment of northern Portugal, high on a hill surrounded by dense woodland, it offers particularly stunning views. The hotel's modern ninety-three rooms and suites are popular among a broad range of guests, appealing to couples, families, business travelers, as well as larger groups attending a conference or celebrating a special occasion. The rooms at the Pena Park Hotel are spacious and tastefully appointed, equipped with modern amenities, and enjoying ample natural light thanks to their stunning floor-to-ceiling windows. Outstanding Portuguese hospitality takes top priority throughout the hotel, but especially so at the Biclaque panoramic restaurant, where local and seasonal ingredients are used to create delicious dishes that put a modern twist on the region's culinary traditions. Weather permitting, you can dine outside on the terrace, sipping a delicious glass of local wine, or lounge in the bar enjoying the peaceful natural surroundings.

Mrs T: "Waking up in the middle of the countryside with a view of the landscape is fantastic. At sunrise you are infused with energy for the day."

Indoor and outdoor activities

The Pena Park Hotel offers so much more than just relaxing hotel accommodation and an exquisite restaurant; it also boasts a number of activities both indoors and outdoors. One of the indoor facilities on offer is a large spa area featuring Finnish sauna, Turkish steam bath, and indoor pool. Quiet areas, wellness massages, detox treatments, and face masks using natural products all ensure guests can totally de-stress and enjoy the views of the surrounding greenery. Those wanting to work on their fitness or build up some muscle instead—or in combination with the wellness treatments—choose a dynamic workout using the modern equipment in the gym. Fresh-air activity options are provided by a large outdoor pool, open during the summer, and guests can also go jogging, hiking, or cycling in the hotel's beautiful natural surroundings all year round. Want to amp things up a little? Then head to the adventure park next-door.

↑ Those who are not satisfied with the four in-house Tesla Destination Chargers, can choose from the 10 Superchargers right next door.

↑ The beauty of northern Portugal is evident in the hotel's immediate surroundings. Hills, forests, and pretty, picturesque little towns create a true picture postcard panorama all year round.

Insight Pena Park Hotel

Located in the middle of the countryside, the hotel puts a particular emphasis on outdoor sports, especially cycling. The hotel team will be pleased to help you plan the best routes and destinations depending on your requirements. Helpful maps and directions can also be provided. If you did not bring your own bike with you, you can of course hire one. Other tailor-made offers for bikers include a special cyclists' massage, detailed tour weather forecasts, and a transfer service from the hotel to your route start and return.

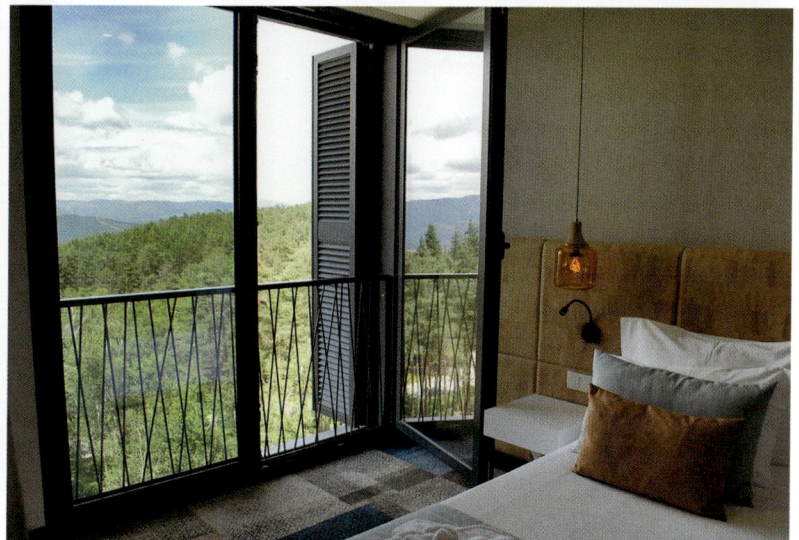

In addition to modern rooms and furnishings, the hotel also boasts a large spa area with indoor and outdoor swimming pools, ↑ as well as a sauna and a gym featuring numerous modern appliances.

AROUND RIBEIRA DE PENA
Portugal

An adventure in Portugal's thinly populated north country

Tras o Montes ("beyond the mountains") is the name of Portugal's northernmost region, and this wild and lonely land indeed seems far from anywhere. You will find here superb scenery and untouched nature, adventure parks and ancient towns and villages—a treasure trove of exciting experiences to be had.

Pena Aventura
(approx. ½ mile/1km)

The Pena Aventura Park, close to the hotel, offers numerous outdoor activities for young and old in its woodlands, thematically organized according to the four elements of air, fire, earth, and water. The Big Air Bungee Ejection, for example, catapults you 50ft (15m) into the air with two giant elastic ropes. You can trounce your enemy in a paintball fight, or race around the mountain bends in the Alpine Coaster bobsleigh. A tall climbing wall and a treetop path wait to be conquered, while the nearby river attracts kayakers and rafters. The highlight for many visitors to the Pena Aventura, however, is the Fantasticable. Suspended from a steel zipline, you'll glide at a height of 490ft (150m) above the valley some 4,900ft (1,500m) from one hilltop to another. At speeds up to 80mph (130km/h), you'll think you are flying!

Guimarães
(approx. 34 miles/55km)

Guimarães, with its UNESCO World Heritage historic center, is a good half hour's drive from the hotel. In 1096, this city became the capital of the County of Portugal and in about 1109, the future first king of Portugal was born here—Afonso I, nicknamed "the Conqueror." Accordingly, Guimarães is considered the "cradle of the Portuguese nationality." The castle and the houses in the narrow

Mr T: "The zipline at the Pena Aventura Park is a top attraction—you're well secured as you 'fly' from one valley to the next. Wow!"

lanes, floodlit at night, along with the picturesque squares, have the makings of a movie set. If time allows, enjoy the spectacular sunset from the highest point of the city in the evening and then dine on fresh fish from the Atlantic in one of the charming tavernas.

Museu do Linho
(approx. 9 miles/15km)

The Linen Museum in the Limões district is a special attraction for visitors with a love of textiles and fabrics. Here you will learn everything about linen weaving, which was once the main commercial activity in the region. In the museum you can see historic spinning wheels and looms as well as numerous fabric

to celebrate

The Festas Gualterianas, initiated to honor St. Gualtern, the patron saint of Guimarães, have been celebrated by thousands of tourists and locals since 1906, always on the first weekend of August. Events include the Procession of the Flax, recalling the local linen-weaving industry, the Battle of the Flowers, and the March Gualteriana, a procession with lavishly decorated wagons.

Festas Gualterianas
Guimarães
early August

patterns, embroidery, tablecloths, and linen sheets. Photos, information boards, and flow charts explain the different processing steps from the harvested flax to the finished linen product. Adjoining the museum is a small showroom where local artisans who work with linen display and sell their work.

Nature Park of Alvão
(approx. 18 miles/29km)

Even the approach to the Parque Natural do Alvão along narrow, winding roads is something of an adventure. Located on the western slope of the Alvão massif, the nature park spans two altitude zones. The lower-lying area near the village of Ermelo, at an altitude of about 1,476ft (450m), is mostly composed of slate, with a largely green landscape. The upper zone near Lamas de Olo, meanwhile, at about 3,280ft (1,000m), is all granite, and high-mountain vegetation dominates here. The Nature Park of Alvão is a refuge for wildlife, including wolves, peregrine falcons and majestic golden eagles—with luck, hikers can observe them from afar. From up close you can enjoy the scenic Fisgas de Ermelo waterfalls, where between tall rocks the Olo River plunges some 820ft (250m) over several cascade steps.

Vila Real
(approx. 28 miles/45km)

A half hour's drive from the hotel takes you to the small town of Vila Real, located on a high plateau and surrounded by the Marão and Alvão mountain ranges. Founded in 1289, the picturesque old town boasts numerous flower-bedecked balconies, the Cathedral of Vila Real, also known as the Church of St. Dominic, and the birthplace of the explorer Diogo Cão (Diogo Cam). In 1482, he was the first European to reach and sail up the mighty Congo River in Africa. The small local Corgo River in Vila Real has a beautiful, inviting waterfront. On a walk through the little town,

↑ One of the most attractive squares in Guimarães is the Largo da Oliveira, with the Igreja de Nossa Senhora da Oliveira church and the medieval city hall. The square is lined with numerous cafés and restaurants, inviting you to relax over a drink and watch the Portuguese world go by.

↑ The blue of the sky and the water, the gray of the rocks, and the ocher hues of the dried vegetation create a superb display of colors at the Fisgas de Ermelo Waterfall, where the Olo River cascades toward the valley.

make sure that you try out some of the local specialties. You can sample sweet dishes, such as *toucinho do céu* ('bacon from heaven,' an almond cake), or savory delicacies including *bolas de carne* (meatballs) and *tripas aos molhos* (pork tripe with sauces).

SIX SENSES DOURO VALLEY

Samodães/Lamego, Portugal

The attractive Six Senses Douro Valley with its panoramic, vineyard views sets new standards in luxury, sustainability and hospitality in one of the world's most outstanding wine regions.

hotel info:

Six Senses Douro Valley
Quinta de Vale Abraão
P-5100-758 Samodães
Tel.: +351 254 660600
Mail: reservations-dourovalley@sixsenses.com
Web: www.sixsenses.com/en/resorts/douro-valley

charging facilities:

1 Tesla DeC (Tesla only)

The Six Senses Douro Valley is located at the source of the river in the heart of the Alto Douro winegrowing region. Originally a 19th-century manor, it has been exquisitely renovated, and now offers every modern amenity. Large windows in the stylish rooms and suites provide breathtaking views over the idyllic hotel park, the vineyards, and the Douro Valley. In addition to the wellness options at the on-site spa, with its indoor and outdoor pool, as well as a fitness and relaxation facility, guests can also learn to make their own beauty products, such as scrubs and masks, or discover the traditional philosophy behind yoga. Hotel manager, Nick

Mrs T: "A pampering culture for all the senses, exceeding our greatest expectations!"

Yarnell, and his team place great emphasis on ensuring guests are not only looked after in a friendly, professional manner, but also that the property itself is run as sustainably as possible. The excellent cuisine incorporates herbs and vegetables from the hotel's organic garden and ingredients sourced from local farmers. It goes without saying that many of the wines at Six Senses are similarly locally produced in the Alto Douro!

AROUND SAMODÃES/LAMEGO
Portugal

Portugal's wine treasure trove on the banks of the Douro

Wine has been produced in the Alto Douro for 2,000 years, and its history colors and shapes the unique cultural landscape of northern Portugal. The Douro River meets the Atlantic at Porto, the city that gave its name to the region's most famous product: port wine.

Museu do Douro
(approx. 4½ miles/7km)

The Douro Museum is located in Peso da Régua, on the other side of the river, just a few minutes from the hotel. It is housed in the former winery and a modern extension. The museum's exhibits center on history, culture, and winegrowing in the Alto Douro region, a UNESCO World Cultural Heritage Site. In addition to the museum, the complex also houses an archive, a wine bar, and a library. After your museum visit, take in the view of the Douro from the terrace at the front of the building, which features a historic wine ship, or continue with a tour of the Memória da Terra do Vinho wine exhibition housed in Warehouse No. 43 on nearby Rua da Ferreirinha.

Lamego (approx. 7 miles/11km)

Lamego is a fifteen-minute drive along the Douro's south bank. Although it is a small town with a population of only 26,000, it is also a Catholic bishop's see, which was officially documented in the year 570, and then again from 1071 onward, following several changes of rule during the days of the Moorish presence on the Iberian Peninsula. The picturesque old town is well worth visiting, with its castle ruins, as well as a number of religious buildings, including the Gothic cathedral, which was heavily remodeled in

Mr T: "The Six Senses also uses a Tesla Model S and so we are certain that our car is in good hands and company."

the 16th and 17th centuries, the bishop's palace, which is today home to the municipal museum, and the Santuário de Nossa Senhora dos Remédios pilgrimage site. Built in rococo style in the mid-18th century, the sanctuary is accessed from the main road via a 686-step double staircase (below).

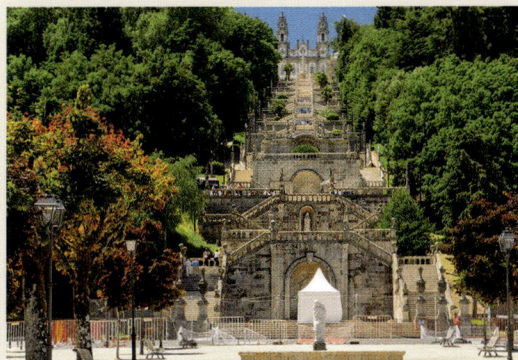

to celebrate

October, when the grape harvest takes place in the Alto Douro region, is also the time of the local wine festivals. In many wine towns and villages, you now have the opportunity to sample port, red, and white wines made from the grapes of earlier years.

Wine festivals in the Alto Douro
October

↑ Beautiful baroque double staircases take you up to the principal floor of the Casa de Mateus. The small palace is surrounded by extensive gardens and a park featuring many invaluable, mature trees.

up to the Casal de Loivos Viewpoint, even in an electric car. However, it is great fun driving along the winding road and the views make up for all the effort. The beautiful vantage point reveals fantastic panoramic vistas over the Douro Valley, with its vineyards, farmsteads, and small villages sprawling along both sides of the river as far as the eye can see. An information panel provides a quick overview. The vastness and tranquility up here are a striking contrast to the hustle and bustle in the narrow lanes down by the river.

Rio Cabrum (approx. 22½ miles/36km)

An hour's drive to the west, the Rio Cabrum, flowing from the south, plunges itself into the Douro. The valley of the 12½ mile (20km) tributary has been partly dammed up to form a small, elongated lake in the lower reaches, but remains largely untouched in the upper parts. It can be accessed via the scenic highway M554-1, which runs parallel to the river, some 1,300 ft (700m) east, before eventually crossing it—now as the M554—right next to a Roman stone bridge between Covelinhas and Ovadas. Covelinhas also provides access to the Cascatas dos Moinhos, where the Rio Cabrum plunges down the canyon steps into a narrow gorge. The waterfalls are popular among canyoneering enthusiasts, who abseil down wearing protective helmets.

Miradouro de Casal de Loivos (approx. 20 miles/32km)

The train stops at a beautiful old station by the Douro in Pinhão, and it is a steep climb

Casa de Mateus (approx. 20 miles/32km)

Is there anyone who hasn't heard of Mateus Rosé? It is an uncomplicated wine, sold in large quantities. Once you've seen the label, you will know what awaits you at the end of a half-hour e-car drive: the Casa de Mateus (above left), situated in the town of the same name near Vila Real. A baroque palace with a large outdoor staircase, the Casa was built in 1745 by Italian architect Nicolau Nasoni. An adjacent chapel dates from the same period. The Casa de Mateus is today owned by a foundation, which aims to promote cultural and scientific activities. The palace's library, some receiving rooms, a small museum, and the wine cellar are all open to the public. A visit to the wine cellar also includes a wine tasting. The chapel and the vast park, with its ancient cedars and a small lake, are equally accessible. The lake beautifully reflects the palace's main façade, and at its center "sleeps" a marble nymph, created by João Cutileiro in 1981.

SPAIN

HACIENDA ZORITA WINE HOTEL & SPA
Valverdón, Spain

The Hacienda Zorita Wine Hotel & Spa is situated in a former monastery looking back on a rich history. Just fifteen minutes from the historic city of Salamanca, it offers a blissful retreat by the Tormes River.

hotel info:

Hacienda Zorita Wine
Hotel & Spa
Ctra. Ledesma, km 10
E-37115 Valverdón
(Salamanca)
Tel.: +34 923 129400
Mail: zorita@
the-haciendas.com
Web: www.
haciendazorita.com

charging facilities:

1 Tesla DeC (Tesla only)
1 Tesla DeC (all EVs)

A former monastery, Hacienda Zorita Wine Hotel & Spa is a beautiful wine resort on the Tormes River dating back to the 14th century. Now beautifully restored, it continues to be a place of rest and contemplation. Guests are immediately greeted at the welcome desk, which not only acts as a reception, but also as the shop for the hotel's homegrown wines. The monks' cells have been elegantly converted into guest rooms, some of which are as large as an average city apartment. Warm earthy tones, natural stone floors, and an abundance of wood pay tribute to the past, while the large bathrooms accentuate the present, and painstaking attention

Mrs T: "*What could be nicer than sitting in the hotel garden while four storks majestically make their rounds and then settle on the roof?*"

to detail rounds off the impressive interiors. With its expansive garden, the Hacienda is in a world all of its own—a world that was even visited by Christopher Columbus, who is said to have gifted the monastery the seeds of the four sequoia trees over 500 years ago that today tower over the property. Equally splendid is the selection of house wines, which can be enjoyed with the delicious, organic dishes served at the restaurant.

AROUND VALVERDÓN
Spain

A barren plateau of austere beauty

The countryside west of Madrid is sparsely populated and barren, then opens out to an impressive 2,625ft (800m) high plateau. Agriculture dominates the area and large reservoirs such as the Almendra Dam with its imposing 636ft (202m) high wall have been constructed to irrigate the dry land.

Salamanca
(approx. 8 miles/13km)

The hotel is located a fifteen-minute drive from more than 2,000 years old Salamanca, a UNESCO World Heritage Site and home to the world's third-oldest university. Its students significantly shape the city's identity—and not just in the medieval center with the university, the two cathedrals, and the vast Plaza Mayor. The latter, a Baroque square with arcaded townhouses, is the finest in Spain. In addition to the ornate city hall, it is home to numerous cafés and restaurants, where the university's many students, locals, and tourists enjoy the unique atmosphere until the early hours. A stroll through the historic center also takes in the *Casa de las conchas*, whose façade is adorned with more than 300 stone shells, and the Roman bridge over the river.

Arribes del Duero Natural Park
(approx. 50 miles/80km)

Driving west from the Hacienda Zorita along the SA-300 and SA-302, through the farming region of the high plateau, your first stop will be the large Almendra Dam. The area west of the dam marks the start of the Parque Natural de Arribes de Duero, a nature reserve extending 50 miles (80km) from north to south. The Duero River here forms the border with Portugal, where it is known as Douro, and the

Mr T: "The Hacienda is a cosmopolitan winery; the Columbus beer brewed here, named 'Coolumbus,' is the perfect proof."

Douro International Natural Park extends on the Portuguese side. With its cork oaks and juniper trees, the parks are a haven for wildlife such as wild cats, genets, badgers, and otters. The Pozo de los Humos waterfall, located in a verdant tributary valley about 1¼ miles (2km) from the Duero, is popular among hikers.

HOSPES PALAU DE LA MAR
Valencia, Spain

Its location near Valencia's historic center makes the charming Hospes Palau de la Mar an ideal design hotel for travelers who want to explore the ancient city on foot.

hotel info:

Hospes Palau de la Mar
Avinguda de Navarro
Reverter, 14
E-46004 Valencia
Tel.: +34 963 162884
Mail: palaudelamar@
hospes.com
Web: www.
hospes.com/palau-mar

charging facilities:

1 Tesla DeC (Tesla only)
1 Tesla DeC (all EVs)

Mr T: "*The car can stay attached to the Destination Charger, because Valencia is the perfect size to be discovered on foot or by bike.*"

A classic 19th-century townhouse situated in the elegant Eixample district of the port city of Valencia houses the Hospes Palau de la Mar. The building has been beautifully renovated; its stunning entrance area is bright white, as are its splendid rooms—including the Dreamer's double room and the exclusive Presidential Suite. The quaint interior courtyard, meanwhile, is a tranquil oasis in the heart of this vibrant city. The attentive staff are only too happy to offer guests recommendations, be it for some of the sights to explore in Valencia, or for the wine to choose at the Ampar restaurant. Head chef Carlos Julián here creates superb paella dishes, for which the region is famed, using fresh vegetables and typically locally-produced Valencian ingredients. If you are only looking for a snack, head to the more casual Ampar lounge bar. The spa facility on the second floor overlooks the interior courtyard. It is complemented by a classic wellness area on the basement level, featuring an indoor Jacuzzi, sauna, steam bath, and gym. The entire complex places great emphasis on using organic and natural products.

AROUND VALENCIA
Spain

A city of contrasts

Everything comes together beautifully in Valencia: old and new, the Moorish and Spanish past, and a rarely found open-mindedness toward modern design. It all forms the background of a vibrant city, home to countless cafés and restaurants, shops, museums, parks, and exhibitions—a great place!

Ciutat Vella (approx. ½ mile/1km)

Just a few minutes' walk from the hotel is the Ciutat Vella, the historic center of Valencia. In the tangle of alleyways and streets, it soon becomes clear that this is a city that never sleeps. Everywhere you look, there are little cafés, restaurants, independent boutiques, and larger stores all bustling with life, not to mention a high concentration of gorgeously restored historic buildings. Outstanding places to visit are the National Museum of Ceramics and Decorative Arts with its spectacular collection, the Gothic Cathedral home to the Holy Chalice (said to be the chalice at the Last Supper), and the picturesque Central Market, or Mercat Central. This Valencian Art Nouveau market hall boasts hundreds of appetizing dishes guaranteed to make your mouth water.

Ciutat de les Arts i les Ciències (approx. 1¼ miles/2km)

It is hard to imagine a greater contrast to Valencia's Old Town than the City of Arts and Sciences designed by architects Santiago Calatrava and Félix Candela in the Turia's dry riverbed. Several white complexes, which appear to consist almost exclusively of circular and elliptical shapes (below), soar out of giant pools of water, which reflect the structures, in a vast expanse of parkland. The complex is home to a science museum, the opera house,

> Mrs T: *"Valencia, a city of many surprises! Living here is everything—historical, stylish, and modern—all at the same time."*

Europe's largest aquarium 1,184,030 sq ft (110,000 sq m), a multipurpose hall, an ultramodern 3D IMAX cinema, a planetarium, and a laserium. It is no surprise then that the Ciutat de les Arts i les Ciències has already been used as a filmset for the movie *Tomorrowland* and the TV series *Doctor Who*.

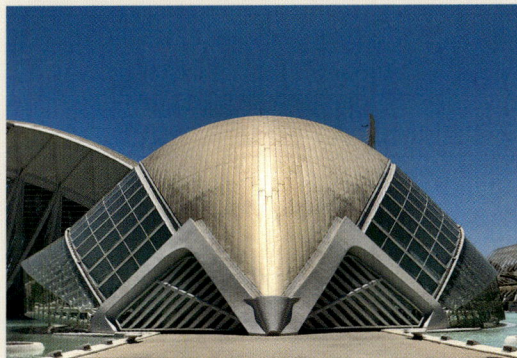

to eat

The Paella Valenciana is considered the national dish of the region and is served on the Spanish Mediterranean coast. The basis is rice, which derives its typical yellow color from saffron. The main ingredients are chicken and rabbit meat, as well as tomatoes, green and white beans. Salt, garlic, and rosemary flavor the dish. You can try the Paella Valenciana in numerous restaurants in the city. In 1992, it even gained an entry in the *Guinness Book of Records*—in a 66ft (20m) diameter pan, a paella was prepared to feed 100,000 people.

Paella Valenciana available anywhere in the city

LA FUENTE DE LA HIGUERA

Ronda, Spain

The Hotel La Fuente de la Higuera is an attractive, family-run gem affording its guests beautiful views of the surrounding, gently rolling Andalusian countryside. Pure relaxation in an idyllic setting.

hotel info:

La Fuente de la Higuera
Partido de los
Frontones S/N
E-29400 Ronda
Tel.: +34 615 690024
Mail: info@
hotellafuente.com
Web: www.
hotellafuente.com

charging facilities:

2 Tesla DeC (Tesla only)
1 Tesla DeC (all EVs)

Hotel La Fuente de la Higuera sits perched atop a hill just a few miles north of the Andalusian town of Ronda. Formerly a finca or country estate, it has been elaborately converted into a stunning, sophisticated boutique hotel by Christina Piek and her family. The rooms and suites are all individually appointed, and the tasteful dark wood furniture complements the traditional style found in Andalusian manors. Antiques and carefully chosen paintings round off the interior, while roses bloom and lemon and orange trees grow outside the windows. With its stately palms, ancient olive trees, and deep-blue pool, the hotel garden is a scene from a romantic

Mr T: "The fact that you can sit under a starry sky at dinner fits in perfectly with the high standard of the cuisine."

dream—a place where you could endlessly gaze out over the rolling landscape from the comfort of the sun loungers. The perfection of the scenery is matched by the delicious food personally prepared by chef Pablo, the owner's son. He uses the best, fresh ingredients, some of which are grown in the hotel's own garden. And for guests who would like to join in there is an honesty bar where they can mix their own after-dinner drinks.

AROUND RONDA
Spain

At the southern end of the Iberian Peninsula

In Andalusia, the traces of the Moorish past are as clearly apparent as nowhere else in Spain. Enchanting Arab-inspired buildings as well as the culture of the oasis-like courtyards take the visitor into an exotic world. In sharp contrast are the mundane Costa del Sol and the British exclave of Gibraltar with its famous macaques.

Ronda
(approx. 6 miles/10km)

With its gleaming white old town, known as La Ciudad, perched atop a rocky plateau, Ronda is considered one of the most beautiful towns in Andalusia. Standing on the cliff edge at the Mirador de Ronda lookout provides a spectacular view over the surrounding landscape. Equally spectacular is the "worm's eye view" you get by descending into the deep Tajo de Ronda gorge, which separates the old from the new town, and from where you can look up at the gigantic 18th-century Puente Nuevo bridge (below right). That period that also gave rise to the rules for modern Spanish bullfighting and the imposing bullring that Ernest Hemingway immortalized in his book, *Death in the Afternoon*. The hip rooftop bar at the neighboring Hotel Catalonia Ronda offers a great, almost bird's-eye view down into the ring.

Gibraltar
(approx. 68 miles/110km)

From Ronda, the scenic highway A-369 running along the westerly Sierra Grazalema massif continues to head south via the A-405 to The Rock—the nickname given to Gibraltar, a British overseas territory since 1713. Upon entering Gibraltar, you soon arrive at the small city center with its Main Street, where everything is very British, and cozy cafés and

Mrs T: "*Our spacious suite has a bathroom with a copper bathtub, an open fireplace, and, best of all, a private terrace.*"

stores abound. The Rock Hotel, boasting the southernmost Tesla Destination Charger in continental Europe, is located in the foothills nearby, while the Barbary macaques frolic around on cliffs reaching heights of 1,398ft (426m) above the city. A cable car takes visitors to the "Rock Apes" habitat.

↑ If you are searching for the epitome of good taste, the Maria Cristina is the right place for you—noble and luxurious, yet never ostentatious. Sumptuous fabric in timelessly beautiful designs convey an unpretentious exclusivity.

HOTEL MARIA CRISTINA

San Sebastián, Spain

Hotel Maria Cristina, in the heart of San Sebastián, delights with the ultimate in luxury and feel-good value. With stunning views over the Cantabrian Sea and Urumea River, the majestic Maria Cristina is a true feast for the senses.

hotel info:

Hotel Maria Cristina
Paseo Republica
Argentina, 4
E-20004 San Sebastián
Tel.: +34 943 437600
Mail: reservations via
the website
Web: www.
theluxurycollection.
com/mariacristina

charging facilities:

1 Tesla DeC (Tesla only)
1 Tesla DeC (all EVs)

The beautiful façade of the Hotel Maria Cristina conjures up images of elegant couples emerging from traditional horse-drawn carriages, delighted to be spending summer in the splendor of this magnificent building with its cream façade and elegant dome. Today, however, a modern Tesla stands in front of the traditional building from La Belle Epoque, and of course it can be charged there too. This fits in perfectly with the philosophy of Ned Capeleris, the hotel's manager who cares deeply about the hotel's proud position in the city and who runs his team like a

Mr T: "The traditional hotel's close connections with the town where it is based, its history and its future, can be felt everywhere."

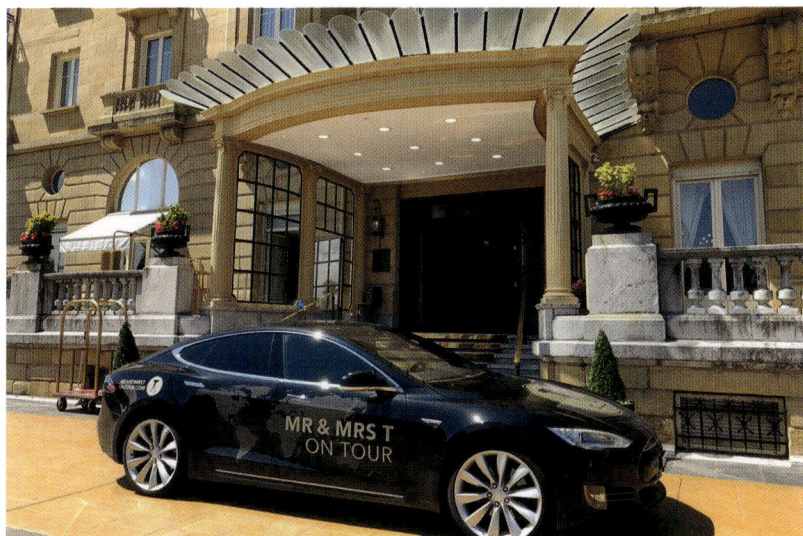

↑ Tesla instead of a horse-drawn carriage—the perfect Maria Cristina is, of course, prepared for guests with an electric drive.

family. And, although this is a luxury hotel, the atmosphere is at the same time warm and welcoming.

Regal and cinematic glamor

The rooms and suites of the Hotel Maria Cristina radiate a royal splendor. The most beautiful are in the round corner rooms under the dome and those with large roof terraces next to the dome, all offering expansive views over the city, the river, and the bay. Movie fans who flock to the city for the annual Film Festival in September enjoy the glamor of the Bette Davis Suite, in which numerous portrait photos recall the legendary Hollywood diva. The DRY San Sebastián, the hotel's bar with a large outdoor terrace, is equally hip and cinematic. The menu includes classic cocktails, such as the "White Russian," and innovative creations, including the "Lost in Translation," which is made from Japanese whiskey and sake. At the DRY Bar you can also try it's signature "Jim-Let Fox-Trot" created by the popular and well-known Mixologist Javier de las Muelas. If you prefer to focus on the food, you will find what you are looking for in the hotel's pop-up restaurant, offering Spanish cuisine, or at Café Saigon, which specializes in Asian food. You can burn off the calories you have consumed in the 1,830sq ft (170sq m) fitness area. State-of-the-art treadmills, fitness bikes, and weight-training equipment are available. This outstanding facility shows once again how perfectly the hotel manages to combine tradition and modernity.

↑ The hotel, equally as imposing as the theater opposite, is located on the Okendo Plaza in the historic district of Parte Zaharra, a few steps away from the city's Urumea River.

Insight Maria Cristina

In keeping with the exquisite luxury and excellent cuisine at the Hotel Maria Cristina, its Bar DRY San Sebastián is one of the most sophisticated venues of its kind. The décor combines the style of the Belle Époque with contemporary glamor. The clever use of ornamental mirrors on the walls, velvet chairs, and leather armchairs make the bar the perfect place to relax (see picture on page 32). The many pictures of movie stars are a reminder of the golden age of the annual San Sebastián Film Festival, which still attracts many top actors today. So there may well be a celebrity mingling with the illustrious guests at this fantastic bar.

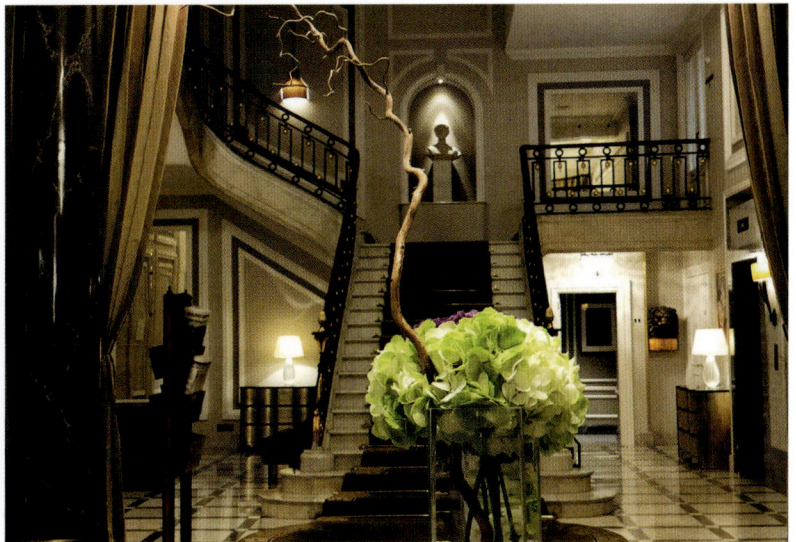

The Maria Cristina achieves top ratings in every respect—high quality furnishings, luxurious rooms and suites, and ↑ outstanding cuisine combine to create the perfect ambience.

AROUND SAN SEBASTIÁN
Spain

What to do in the Basque Country

Situated only 12½ miles (20km) from the border with France, the capital of the Spanish Basque region charms with its superb location in the beautiful bay of La Concha and an abundance of great gastronomic treats on offer—a truly unforgettable feast for eyes and palate!

to eat

On hearing the name Akelarre, connoisseurs' hearts have been beating faster for almost half a century: San Sebastián's legendary gourmet restaurant, in existence since 1970, has gradually acquired and maintained three Michelin stars since 2006. Pedro Subijana and his team cook fish and seafood in constantly evolving, inspiring variations for their guests, who can also choose from 650 top wines from around the world. Since moving to new premises in the Igueldo district in 2017, diners have also been able to enjoy the most beautiful panoramic views.

Akelarre
Padre Orcolaga, 56
(Igeldo)
www.akelarre.net/en/

Playa de La Concha
(approx. ½ mile/1km)

It's just ten minutes walk from the hotel to Playa de La Concha, which is considered one of the most beautiful city beaches in the world. About 4,265ft (1,300m) long and on average 130ft (40m) wide, the beach extends in an almost perfect—as the name implies: shell-shaped—arch along the eponymous Bahia de Santa Clara. What the bay and the island are for surfers, windsurfers, and paragliders, the beach is for bathers, strollers, beach volleyball players. The Paseo, which runs along the entire beach, with its elegant hotels, apartment houses, and cafés, is for flâneurs: a little paradise. And to make this earthly bliss even more perfect, the 1,640ft (500m) long Playa de Ondarreta adjoins it to the west.

Palacio de Miramar
(approx. 1¼ miles/2km)

The Palacio de Miramar is a former royal summer palace situated on the small promontory that separates the Playa de La Concha from the next beach. The British architect

Ralph Selden Wornum designed this English-style palace with neo-Gothic elements, on the orders of Maria Cristina, widow of King Alfonso XII. It was completed in 1893. After the death of the queen dowager in 1929, the palace went to her son King Alfonso XIII, before the Second Republic confiscated the

Mrs T: "The hotel team's warm welcome at the Maria Cristina makes you feel as if you've been here one hundred times before."

building in 1931. In 1958, the Franco regime finally returned the Palacio de Miramar to Alfonso's son, Don Juan, who sold it to the city in 1972. Today, the royal rooms and the garden can be visited, and the university uses part of the building for its summer school.

Parte Zaharra
(approx. ½ mile/1km)

The historic old town of San Sebastián—Donostia in Basque—lies between the Bahia de La Concha in the west, the Monte Urgull, rising steeply out of the sea in the north, and the Urumea River in the east, all within walking distance from the hotel. The name is a mix of the Spanish Parte Vieja and the Basque Alde

Zaharra, both meaning "old town." The district, burned down in 1813 and later rebuilt, made up the actual city until the demolition of the city walls in 1862. Today, the lanes with the flower-adorned houses surrounding the Plaza de la Constitutión are a popular place to spend the evening. Numerous bars serve the popular tapas-style *pintxos de Donostia*, a specialty of the region, which are served cold or hot as small appetizers. Enjoy an authentic experience and go on a culinary journey of discovery through the Old Town. In each bar, select a few of these delicious morsels, have a drink, and then move on to the next the next pintxo and enjoy more delicious Basque specialties. Or you can simply join one of the guided pintxos tours—your hotel will be happy to give you more information.

Guggenheim Museum, Bilbao (approx. 62 miles/100km)

Those who prefer a more modern experience instead of an old-world charm will find exactly what they're looking for in Bilbao, only 90 minutes' drive away. The truly sensational "new" Guggenheim was designed by Frank O. Gehry and completed in 1997. It is home to a permanent exhibition of contemporary sculptures, installations, and video art, as well as constantly changing exhibitions around various themes. Architecture and art are combined here in an incredibly exciting way—a definite must-see experience!

Aquarium (approx. 1¼ miles/2km)

San Sebastián's Aquarium is located to the northwest of the fishing port, in a building set into the steep coast. Spain's first natural science museum, it can be reached on foot from the hotel in just over 20 minutes and is open every day. In addition to a large variety of tropical fish, seahorses and loggerhead turtles, moray eels and stingrays cavort in the aquarium's pools. Particularly impressive are

↑ The Playa de La Concha is one of the most attractive city beaches anywhere in the world. The access to the open sea from the crescent-shaped bay is "guarded" by the two rocky massifs of Monte Igueldo on the left and Monte Urgull on the right.

↑ Pintxos are the hallmark of Basque cuisine. Although similar to tapas, they are often small kebabs (hence the name—Spanish "pinchos" means skewer). The small treats are usually served on a small slice of bread. The range of variations is huge—so you may not be able to try them all, even if you are tempted.

the majestic sharks in the main basin, which holds 660,400 gallons (2.5 million liters) of water. A spectacular glass tunnel takes visitors right through the center of the tank.

MAS FALGARONA

Avinyonet de Puigventós/Figueres, Spain

The Mas Falgarona Hotel & Spa is a charming and stylish house in the middle
of the Catalan countryside, close to the French border. Its natural surroundings
under the Empordà sky promise a relaxing stay.

hotel info:

Mas Falgarona
Carrer de Llers, s/n
E-17742 Avinyonet de
Puigventós (Girona)
Tel.: +34 972 546628
Mail: info@
masfalgarona.com
Web: www.
masfalgarona.com

charging facilities:

1 Tesla DeC (Tesla only)
1 Tesla DeC (all EVs)

The approach to Mas Falgarona Hotel & Spa, near the town of Figueres, capital of the Alt Empordà region in the north of Catalonia, takes you up a narrow cypress-lined lane. Located in a lush, natural setting, this boutique hotel is housed in stunning 15th-century buildings featuring designer furniture and meticulously chosen finishing touches. Each of the fourteen rooms has been individually appointed to the highest of standard—the Villa Deluxe also has its own kitchen. Max is the perfect host, proudly claiming that Mas Falgarona has adopted a "Tesla mentality," when he speaks about the property's unique design. And nowhere is this

Mr T: *"At the Mas Falgarona
we enjoy our breakfast in the
lush nature, under a palm tree
by the pool while listening to the
twittering of the birds."*

design more apparent than at the hotel's spa facility, featuring indoor pool, sauna, relaxation and treatment rooms, all perfectly integrated into a traditional stone barn. You can also enjoy simply lying by the outdoor pool and soaking up sun and nature. The Mas Falgarona places great emphasis on food quality, serving the finest local produce (including from the hotel's own organic vegetable garden) matched with excellent regional wines.

AROUND FIGUERES
Spain

The wild coast of Catalonia

Forget the traditional sandy beaches and hotel complexes associated with the Costa Brava's tourist resorts of Lloret de Mar and Blanes. The Catalan coastline near Figueres is rocky, interspersed with many small and very beautiful coves and beaches with crystal clear, blue waters, some only accessible by boat.

Teatre-Museu Dalí
(approx. 4¼ miles/7km)

The hotel is located just a few miles out of Figueres, birthplace of the Spanish painter, Salvador Dalí. The town's former municipal theater, where the future Surrealist maestro held his first exhibition, has housed the Dalí Theater-Museum since 1974. It is the world's largest Surrealist building, and was designed down to the finest detail by Dalí himself. Over twenty rooms showcase some 1,500 artworks painted by Dalí throughout his entire career—ranging from Impressionism to Futurism and Cubism to Surrealism. Around every corner, visitors are met by bizarre perspectives, new angles, optical illusions, and other image and photo subjects attesting to his incredible creativity. The crypt in which Salvador Dalí is buried is also open to the public.

Girona
(approx. 29 miles/47km)

The provincial capital, Girona, is a forty-five minute drive away, and the route along the N-II, running parallel to the highway, is the most scenic option for this journey. Home to some 100,000 people, the city is known for its modern university and historic center on the Onyar River, where the impressive Santa Maria Cathedral is also located. From here, it is just a few steps to the picturesque Rambla

Mrs T: "The hotel is ideally located for a pleasant stopover on the drive south as well as a starting point for bike rides and hikes."

de la Libertad, with its many cafés, excellent restaurants, and boutique shops. On the other side of the Onyar, meanwhile, it is worth visiting the Museu del Cinema, whose great collection of often bizarre exhibits on cinematic history would most certainly have met with Salvador Dalí's approval.

to eat

One of Girona's celebrated restaurants is El Celler de Can Roca, run by the three Roca brothers since 1986—chef Joan, dessert guru Jordi, and sommelier Josep. Their reinterpretation of Catalan cuisine was rewarded with three Michelin stars, and the brothers have also received numerous other awards and international fame.
El Celler de Can Roca
Can Sunyer, 48
E-17007 Girona
www.cellercanroca.com

LA TORRE DEL VISCO
Fuentespalda/Teruel, Spain

La Torre del Visco is a wonderful green oasis of peace between Barcelona and Valencia. Relax in the hotel, surrounded by a magnificent decorative garden and the hotel's own farmland.

hotel info:

La Torre del Visco
Partida Torre del
Visco s/n
E-44587 Fuentespalda
Teruel
Tel.: +34 978 769015
Mail: reservas@
torredelvisco.com
Web: www.
torredelvisco.com

charging facilities:

1 Tesla DeC (Tesla only)
1 Tesla DeC (all EVs)

The approach to La Torre del Visco is a highlight in its own right, with the road snaking its way through a breathtakingly wild landscape. The hotel itself is a 15th-century *torre* or tower that has been converted into a delightful patch of paradise. The only inhabited property in the entire valley, it is surrounded by 220 acres (100ha) of its own farmland, where olive and almond trees and other organic produce, such as seasonal fruit and vegetables, are grown. Jemma Markham and her team pull out all the stops to cater to their guests in the sixteen rooms and suites, which measure up to 860 sq ft (80sq m). Embracing sustainability is a top priority for

Mrs T: "When you look along the wide valley or into the spectacular flower garden you'll feel like a princess in her dream prince's castle."

the owner, and so the hotel not only boasts two Tesla Destination Charger, but also has its own on-site water source and is a certified organic farm. Produce from the farm finds its way into the multi-functional hotel kitchen, which operates simultaneously as a breakfast room, common area, and even reception. So you are free to relax and engage in some friendly chat with other hotel guests while watching the chefs prepare the exquisite meals.

AROUND FUENTESPALDA
Spain

A journey of discovery in historic Aragón

Spain's historical ancestral region of Aragón is also one of the greenest areas in the country, home to vast forests. The terrain ranges from the highest mountains in the Pyrenees to the Iberian System mountain range in the south—guaranteeing you an enjoyable CO_2-free trip.

Valderrobres
(approx. 3¾ miles/6 km)

Located just a few minutes' drive north, the historic center of the small town of Valderrobres (meaning "valley of the oaks"), dominates the valley with its impressive row of buildings facing the Rio Matarraña. The Puente de Piedra stone bridge and the San Roque gate lead into the narrow lanes and the Gothic Santa María la Mayor Church, which was modeled on Tarragona Cathedral. The Castillo, perched on the highest point of Valderrobres' town center, dates back to the Middle Ages. Adjacent to these two buildings stands the museum, which highlights regional history and houses a collection of historic costumes, as well as a permanent exhibition dedicated to Elvira de Hidalgo, the Valderrobres-born opera singer and singing teacher of the legendary soprano, Maria Callas.

Salto de la Portellada
(approx. 3¾ miles/6km)

The landscape around the Portellada Waterfall (right) evokes the Wild West we know from the movies. The waters of El Salt ("the jump," as it is also known) cascade 66ft (20m) over the shimmering red rock overhangs to form a small, crystal-clear lake below. The flow of the water depends on the seasons—it may be a torrid stream or run

Mr T: "Sitting comfortable in the library in the evening, watching the fire crackle and listening to classical music—that's life!"

completely dry. Note also the curious rock shapes formed over time. The waterfall is only a short fifteen-minute drive from the hotel if you want to take a dip in the chilly waters. Alternatively, El Salt also acts as the start and end point for a number of signposted hikes throughout the nearby countryside.

to celebrate
On January 17, the city of Valderrobres celebrates its patron, San Antón. To honor the saint, a large campfire is lit on the eve of the feast day, and the town's Christmas tree is burned. On the day itself, the fire's embers are used to grill sausages. The day is a popular local holiday.

La fiesta de
San Antonio Abad
www.valderrobres.es
January 17

↑ The Salto de la Portellada waterfall is one of the area's most stunning beauty spots. Its roaring waters offer a captivating natural place for mindfulness and meditation.

↑ The hotel is the ideal environment to recharge your batteries. Enjoy delightful vistas of untouched nature from the terrace, just beyond the hotel is the enchanting Sierra de Mariola Natural Park.

MASQI – THE ENERGY HOUSE

Banyeres de Mariola, Spain

In the seclusion of the Spanish Sierra de Mariola, the MasQi–The Energy House with its wellbeing and sustainability concept is the perfect place to switch off and recharge your own batteries.

hotel info:

MasQi – The Energy House
Camino de la Mallaeta, s/n
E-03450 Banyeres de Mariola (Alicante)
Tel.: +34 965 567232
Mail: info@masqi.es
Web: www.masqi.es

charging facilities:

1 Tesla DeC (Tesla only)
1 Tesla DeC (all EVs)

You don't have to be able to speak Spanish or Chinese to understand the concept of MasQi–The Energy House, but the boutique hotel's name is certainly apt: *mas* is Spanish for "more" and *qi* Chinese for "energy" or "breath," translating together as "more energy!" When the owner, Sonia Ferre, began converting the 19th-century country estate, located high in the mountains between Alicante and Valencia, into a new hotel, she wanted to create a center where all her guests could replenish their energy and forget those everyday cares. The tranquil environment on the edge of the Sierra de Mariola Nature Park is the ideal base for this, and the meticulously designed hotel, with its eight rooms and suites, provide the perfect setting. Room names such as Shanti, Om, and Namaste bear reference to the most important aspect of MasQi–The Energy House: the idea of incorporating Far Eastern philosophy to increase guests' wellbeing.

Special yoga and meditation in the garden

Sonia Ferre and her team run daily yoga and meditation classes in a specially built, light-filled poolside space known as The Dome. Traditional yoga is complemented with newer concepts, such as the fascially oriented bow-spring. Hearing only the soft twittering of the birds in the garden as you exercise or meditate allows you to literally feel your inner batteries slowly recharging. And as you gaze out across the valley, you can immerse your mind in the rolling vastness of the natural landscape, grounding you in the here and now. The regional ingredients used in the Energy House's kitchen are all as natural as possible—eco-friendly, organic, vegan, and macrobiotic. The day's culinary program starts in the morning with delicious, freshly baked bread and unsweetened jam for breakfast, and ends in the evening at the hotel restaurant, with such international classics as Thai couscous, falafels, or sea bass with shrimp and hot pepper, all freshly prepared. Later in the evening, sipping tea on the terrace under a starry sky, you will feel at total peace in body, mind, and spirit.

Mrs T: "With its fantastic program of wellness treatments, the MasQi is the Supercharger among the Destination Charging hotels!"

↑ The impressive yoga shala, The Dome, by the swimming pool is the ideal place to balance the energy you gained during your yoga practice.

AROUND BANYERES DE MARIOLA
Spain

Inland from the coastal towns of Valencia and Alicante

Spain's scenic diversity opens out in front of you like a picture book. From the palm-fringed beaches of the Mediterranean to the hills of the Sierra de Mariola, picturesque towns and quiet, forested areas invite you to rest and recharge your batteries.

Castillo de Banyeres
(approx. 2 miles/3km)

The Castillo de Banyeres sits on top of the Tossal de l'Aguila ("Eagle Hill") right in the heart of Banyeres de Mariola. The fortress complex was built by the Almohads in the 12th century to protect the town in the north-east of Moorish Andalusia against the Christian troops from Aragón, who were advancing south on their way to reconquer the country. Preserved to this day are the Castillo's main solid, square, 56ft (17m) high watchtower and its two asymmetrical surrounding walls. A cistern was built to supply drinking water in the event of a siege—and a siege did happen in 1248, when King James I's troops captured the Castillo and the town. The castle can be visited on weekends.

Mills along the Rio Vinalopó
(approx. 2½ miles/4km)

Between the 18th and 20th centuries, paper mills around Banyeres de Mariola were powered by the Vinalopó River, allowing the town to achieve a modest wealth with paper manufacture. When local industry was no longer able to keep up with the competition, the mills slowly began to fall into disrepair, and today serve as beautiful examples of industrial architecture. Starting at the southern edge of Banyeres de Mariola, you can follow the approximately 1¼ mile (2km) Ruta

Mr T: "It's great that you can start directly from MasQi–The Energy House for long walks in the nature park."

de los Molinos to Molí l'Ombria, the oldest of the mills, Molí Sol, and Molí Pont. Traveling a few miles farther up the Rio Vinalopó will take you to its source in the Sierra de Mariola.

Sierra de Mariola National Park
(approx. ½ mile/1km)

First opened in 2002, the Sierra de Mariola National Park, spanning an area of about 10½ x 6¼ miles (17 x 10km), starts just east of Banyeres de Mariola and the hotel. Several of its limestone mountains reach heights of over 3,280ft (1,000m), the tallest being Montcabrer at 4,557ft (1,389m). With its vast pine, yew, and holly oak forests, the national park is criss-crossed by numerous hiking trails, including the popular GR 7 long-distance path from the French border to Andalusia. Like the climate itself, the flora and fauna are Mediterranean, and botany enthusiasts will discover an extraordinary park where more than 200 species of fragrant herbs and medicinal plants thrive.

Cava Gran de Agres (approx. 9 miles/15 km)

A 20-minute drive away, near the town of Agres on the edge of the Sierra de Mariola, is a true gem of economic and cultural history in the form of the Cava Gran de Agres. The artificial cave dates back to the 19th century, when there was no electricity, let alone electric fridges. In winter, snow from the Sierra Nevada mountains would be brought by workers to this cave, which is actually a round, multi-story silo embedded into the hillside. The snow would be compacted and stored to make ice, which was being kept well insulated in the process. The ice would be cut into large blocks, loaded onto donkeys, and transported overnight down to Valencia and Alicante on the Mediterranean coast. This means of ice transportation continued well into the 20th century.

Alicante (approx. 25 miles/40km)

With your EV, you can enjoy a scenic route on the one-hour drive from the hotel to the Mediterranean coastal town of Alicante, home to a population of around 330,000. A wide, popular sandy beach extends northeast of the large marina, which is also home to a casino. The modern city center lies farther inland, beyond the prestigious hotels and apartment blocks of the palm-lined Explanada de España. A little to the north stands the great co-cathedral of San Nicolás de Bari, built in the Herrera style of the Spanish Renaissance, and a few steps from there is the picturesque Barrio de la Santa Cruz old town district, often simply called

↑ The Castillo de Banyeres was built in the 13th century as an Almohad fortress to ward off Christian reconquerors. Today, it is the main attraction in the region, welcoming tourists of all religions. The irregular complex was built directly onto the rocks, but despite its fortifications, it eventually succumbed to the onslaught of troops from the north.

↑ The wavy floor mosaic on the Explanada de España in Alicante, consisting of more than six and a half million individual stones, was laid in the 1950s. The promenade is lined with four rows of palm trees and has become one of Alicante's most popular landmarks.

El Barrio. It is a 545ft (166m) climb from the Barrio up to the Castillo de Santa Bárbara, but your efforts will be rewarded with great panoramic views of the entire surrounding landscape.

FRANCE

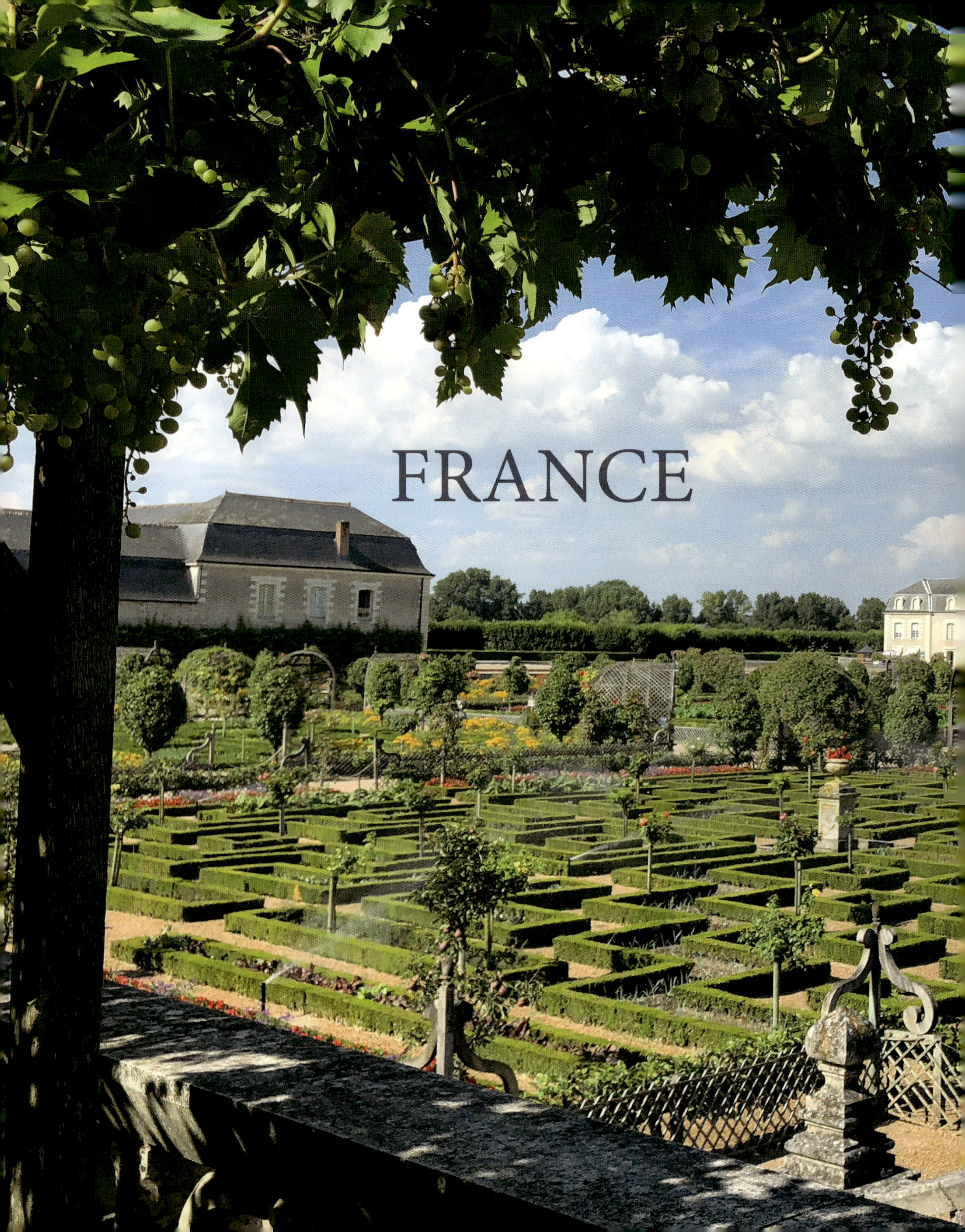

↑ The imposing entrance to the stately main building, which resembles a classic Loire château, is an indication of the hotel's elegance and thanks to the excellent service, you will immediately feel welcome as a guest.

DOMAINE DE LA TORTINIÈRE

Veigné, France

The Domaine de la Tortinière near Tours offers the utmost comfort in a 19th-century château that has been lovingly and beautifully restored and transformed into a unique hotel destination.

hotel info:

Domaine de la
Tortinière
10 Route de Ballan
F-37250 Veigné
Tel.: +33 247 343500
Mail: contact@
tortiniere.com
Web: www.
tortiniere.com

charging facilities:

1 Tesla DeC (Tesla only)
1 Tesla DeC (all EVs)

Situated on a gentle slope a mere fifteen-minute drive south of Tours is an elegant château which houses the Domaine de la Tortinière. Surrounded by 37 acres (15ha) of parkland with ancient Lebanon cedars and redwood trees, the third generation family-run property, managed by Xavier and Anne Olivereau, is a veritable dream come true. The chateau is world-famous—notable guests at the Domaine have included President George Pompidou, writer Françoise Sagan, and actors Audrey Hepburn and Gérard Depardieu. The four-star hotel has twenty-six rooms and suites, located in the château itself, in the adjacent Renaissance pavilion, or in the historic coach house. The exquisitely renovated and classically appointed rooms feature all the modern conveniences expected today, which guarantee to make your stay at the Domaine de la Tortinière a relaxing experience—as well as the perfect base for visiting the world-famous nearby châteaux in the Loire Valley.

Mrs T: "My favorite spot is the swing in the château's lovely park from which you have great views of the pool and the Indre Valley."

Feeling like the lady or the lord of the château

Even the smaller rooms, which bear such telling names as Charme, Prestige, and Elegance, are so carefully and delightfully appointed, that you will instantly feel like a president, actor, or lady/lord of the château. And the suites are even more splendid. There is an equally grand and wonderfully large outdoor pool in the magnificent, park-like garden to the rear of the château. The hotel even puts a rowing boat at their guests' disposal. The restaurant, which is housed in the château's orangery and overlooks the park, is run by head-chefs Jean-Baptiste Drey-Blum and Damien Piochon. Two styles of meals are sevred here: either simple and delicious bistro food, or more sophisticated culinary creations featuring regional ingredients from the Touraine province, including the famous goat's cheese, of course, paired with vintage wines recommended by the in-house sommelier. End the day over a glass of Cognac or Armagnac in the cozy bar with its open fire and billiards table.

↑ You will feel like the lord or lady of the manor in this beautiful château with its stucco decoration and parquet flooring.

AROUND VEIGNÉ
France

In the heart of France

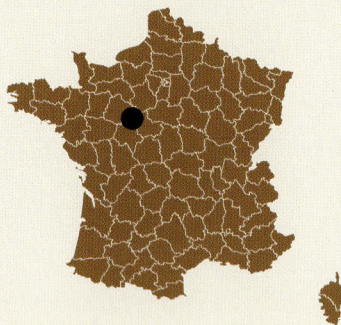

The Loire flows from the Massif Central to the north, then turns west in a large arc before reaching the Atlantic. It is the main artery of this region southwest of Paris, with picturesque châteaux, the country's most historically important cities, and vast stretches of fertile land.

Tours (approx. 9 miles/15km)

Situated some twenty minutes' drive north of the hotel, the city of Tours lies on the Loire River. Its name refers to the Celtic Turones who settled here before the Romans. In the early Middle Ages, Tours was a Frankish town, and it was here that the Frankish leader, Charles Martel, secured the crucial victory over the Moors in the Battle of Tours in 732. In the 1,000 years that followed, the city continued to be fought over, and also served as a base for military campaigns—by Nordic Vikings, Anglo-French rulers, French Catholics, Protestant Huguenots, and, after 1789, revolutionaries. City center attractions include the Cathedral of Saint-Gatien, with its Gothic tower topped with Renaissance spires, and the Archbishop's Palace, which houses a museum of fine arts.

Château and Gardens of Villandry (approx. 19 miles/30km)

After about half an hour's drive northwest from Veigné, you will reach one of the many châteaux on the Loire for which this region is famous: the Château de Villandry. Aside from the impressive Renaissance château itself, however, its mainly the gardens that make Villandry so special. The entire terrain is landscaped and laid out on three levels. On the highest level are the terraced areas right by the castle, including the Sun Garden and the Water Garden, whose waters are distributed

Mr T: "Enjoying an excellent menu on the terrace in the evening, under the open sky, that's truly the good life …"

throughout the grounds via channels. On the middle level are the ornamental gardens, which bear such lovely names as "Garden of Love" and "Music Garden." The ornamental vegetable garden, which once served to supply food for the inhabitants of the château, is at the lowest level. It is fully committed to sustainable and organic gardening.

Château de Chenonceau (approx. 19 miles/30km)

From the hotel, a twenty-minute drive takes you to Château de Chenonceau, one of the finest of the Loire châteaux. The Renaissance masterpiece on the Cher, a tributary of the Loire, comprises three sections—the Tour

to celebrate

Every year, some 30 landscape artists from around the world create contemporary gardens, each with its own theme, in the grounds of Château Chaumont-sur-Loire. These living works of art grow and evolve during the six months from April to November while they are on show. The rules state that the garden should be at its most beautiful in the fall. Visitors wander along the paths of the park as in an open-air museum of contemporary landscape art.

Festival International des Jardins, Le Château F-41150 Chaumont-sur-Loire www.domaine-chaumont.fr April–November

des Marques, the living quarters, and the gallery—as well as two gardens. The Tour des Marques is what remains of a medieval castle on an artificial island on the northern banks of the Cher. The living quarters—the actual château—date back to between 1515 and 1522, and were built a short way farther south in the middle of the river on the foundations of an old mill. Until 1559, the château was connected to a bridge commissioned by Diane de Poitiers, the mistress of Henry II, who also ordered the construction of the Renaissance garden in the east. Following the king's death, his widow, Catherine de Medici, banished her rival from the château. She commissioned her own Renaissance garden at the western end in 1563, and finally had a gallery built over the bridge between 1570 and 1576.

Maison Musée René Descartes (approx. 25 miles/40km)

The small town of Descartes, on the shores of the Creuse River, is an easy half-hour's drive from your hotel. Since 1967, it has borne the name of philosopher and mathematician René Descartes, who was born in 1596 in what was then known as La Haye en Touraine. His birthplace was converted into a small museum in 1974, which is open from early April to late October. The exhibition casts the life and works of one of the modern era's first great philosophers in the historic and cultural context of the Renaissance, displaying a number of original texts and prints.

Salle d'exposition Les Halles, Azay-le-Rideau (approx. 15 miles/25 km)

Azay-le-Rideau, situated barely twenty minutes' drive west of the hotel, is best known for its moated castle. Just a short walk from the castle, another gem in the form of the Showroom Les Halles. Measuring only 1,830sq ft (170sq m), the art gallery was renovated in 2017, and has been showcasing small but outstanding exhibitions of national acclaim ever since. These

↑ The old town of Tours boasts many preserved old buildings, some dating back to the 16th century. In 2014, Place Plumerau was voted "France's most beautiful square in which to enjoy an apéritif." Something worth checking out during your visit.

↑ Where there used to be a medieval castle, one of the most beautiful moated châteaux on the Loire was built during the Renaissance: the Château d'Azay-le-Rideau. The elegant exterior is mirrored inside by the magnificent staircase dating from the time of the château's construction.

have included a retrospective on Salvador Dalí, a solo exhibition on the classic French cartoon series *Les Shadoks*, and a collective exhibition of the work of painters, sculptors, and photographers exploring the theme of *La Nuit* ("the night")."

HÔTEL LES HARAS
Strasbourg, France

The Hôtel Les Haras in Strasbourg in Alsace was established in the premises of a former stud farm and riding stables, which have since become a small oasis of peace in the middle of the city.

hotel info:

Hôtel Les Haras
23 Rue des Glacières
F-67000 Strasbourg
Tel.: +33 390 205000
Mail: via the contact
form on the website
Web: www.les-haras-
hotel.com

charging facilities:

2 Tesla DeC (Tesla only)
1 Tesla DeC (all EVs)

A short stroll south of Strasbourg's historic center, the Hôtel Les Haras and the brasserie of the same name are housed in a former National Stud Farm, so it is no surprise that horses are a running theme throughout the property. You will find horses on the hotel logo, wooden horses, paintings of horses on the walls, and even a large rocking horse in the reception area. The interior décor and furnishings follow in a similar vein; rooms feature wooden floors and leather upholstery, making generous use of timber and natural materials to create a very homely vibe—the perfect place to retreat to after a day out in the vibrant city center. Even the best hotels,

Mr T: "As a former horse stud, the hotel even has a wagon master who likes to take the Tesla to its place in the 'stable' by the Destination Charger."

however, would be nothing without courteous, helpful staff, and Les Haras also excels in this department, from the reception, where guests are offered insider tips, to the on-site brasserie, where Michelin-star chef Marc Haeberlin performs his magic. And no matter which of the chef's specialty dishes you choose, the attentive waitstaff will suggest wines from the extensive cellar to perfectly complement your meal.

↑ The bronze figure of a horse in the middle of the couryard reminds us that the hotel was once a stud farm.

AROUND STRASBOURG
France

The most European of French cities

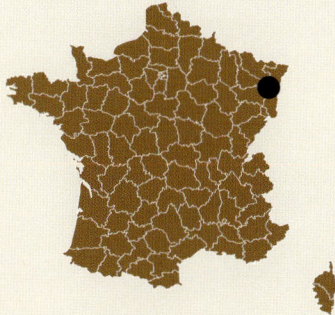

Strasbourg is the ultimate European city. Situated on the French–German border with a history shared by both nations, it is now the seat of the European Parliament, the democratic chamber of the European Union and testament to the spirit of international understanding and tolerance that now prevails.

Strasbourg Cathedral
(approx. ½ mile/1km)

"My soul was filled with a tremendous, indelible impression," so wrote Goethe when he first saw Strasbourg Cathedral in the heart of Strasbourg's historic center, known as La Grande Île. The cathedral, a fifteen-minute walk from the hotel, was built in 1176 to 1439 from pink Vosges sandstone, and fuses Romanesque elements in its eastern section with Gothic style at its western end. One of its most striking features is the 466ft (142m) north tower on the western façade—the tallest structure in the world until 1874. Plans were also drafted for a south tower, but work was never completed. The large rose window in this western façade is one of the most impressive in Europe, letting a soft light fall into the plain central nave.

Strasbourg Neustadt
(approx. 2 miles/3 km)

The district known as Neustadt ("New Town") lies north-east of the Grande Île, the historic center, with which it has conjointly been listed as a UNESCO World Heritage Site since 2017.

The district was built between 1871 and 1914, when Strasbourg was the capital of what was then German Alsace-Lorraine. With its boulevards, squares, and parks, it is now considered the largest collection of German *Gründerzeit* architecture, although the urban design

Mrs T: "At the Brasserie, we indulge in culinary delights, floating in the proverbial seventh–gourmet–heaven."

was actually inspired by Haussmann's plans for Paris. The heart of the district then was Kaiserplatz (Place de la République), its imperial palace (Palais du Rhin), the university and the regional parliament, with the wide Kaiser-Wilhelm-Strasse (Avenue de la Liberté) from the palace to the university plaza.

to drink

Secret Place, a bar in Strasbourg's historic center, is literally an insider tip—the only access is through the pizzeria Aedaen Place. Inside, once you've walked through a "magic wall," you'll be amazed and pleased to find that you have slipped through the small entrance to the famous backyard bar. Reading the fairytale-like cocktail menu is exciting, as are the enchanting drinks conjured up by the professional bar staff.

Secret Place
4-6 rue des Aveugles
www.aedaen-place.com

↑ Strasbourg's old town is the epitome of peace and tranquility, with its picturesque canals and numerous half-timbered houses.

KUBE SAINT-TROPEZ HOTEL
Gassin, France

The Kube Saint-Tropez, located in one of the most elegant and glamorous resorts on the Côte d'Azur, is a destination where not only lovers of modern design and e-car drivers will feel at home.

Mrs T: "The fantastic views over the Gulf of Saint-Tropez and the bar on the hotel's roof terrace convey an upscale, Mediterranean lifestyle."

hotel info:

Kube Saint-Tropez Hotel
319 Route du Littoral
F-83580 Gassin
Tel.: +33 494 972000
Mail: kubehotel@machefert.com
Web: www.kubehotel-saint-tropez.com

charging facilities:

2 Tesla DeC (Tesla only)
1 Tesla DeC (all EVs)

Directly overlooking the Gulf of Saint-Tropez, the five-star Kube Saint-Tropez resort is aptly named, for it features a cubic layout and design. The forty-three rooms in the main building are extremely bright and ultra-stylish, striking a contrast with the darker corridors. There are twenty-seven rooms in the complex's five small villas, whose theme was developed around warm, wooden tones. The attractive garden, with its mature pine trees, features three swimming pools, one of which is an infinity pool that appears to flow directly into the Gulf of Saint-Tropez, with its many colorful yachts. Take advantage of this breathtaking setting to swim a few laps or relax on the sun loungers to the sound of chilled tunes. The pool bar and rooftop terrace bar serve snacks and drinks, while the Marius restaurant's menu includes exquisite international delicacies. You can burn off any surplus calories by heading to the gym for a workout. Tesla travelers will love the wide range of e-bikes, e-scooters, and even electric golf carts on offer—it goes without saying that there are three Destination Chargers on site.

AROUND SAINT-TROPEZ
France

Soaking up sun, art, and high society

The Côte d'Azur is associated with a glamorous lifestyle and Saint-Tropez, a pretty town situated in beautiful countryside, is the most famous resort of all. There are, of course, the yachts of the super-rich, yet the aura of its artistic past creates a pleasantly nostalgic contrast and an agreeable ambience.

Port of Saint-Tropez
(approx. 1¼ miles/2km)

"Seeing and being seen" has been the motto of Saint-Tropez (below) since the 1950s, when the fishing village suddenly became world famous thanks to Roger Vadim's film *And God Created Woman*, starring Brigitte Bardot. In the summer months especially, the millionaires on their yachts and the idlers in the cafés on the promenade create a special ambience—and as if to prove that life can be like a movie, a street artist often prances around wearing the uniform seen in the Louis de Funès film *The Troops of Saint-Tropez*. If you want a bit of peace and quiet, it's a short walk to the pier and its castles, built as part of the coastal defence for the town. Oblivious to the glamor, the fishermen with their small boats simply concentrate on their work, as they did before the film folk arrived.

Plage de Pampelonne
(approx. 5 miles/8km)

From the hotel, you drive across the hilly peninsula on which Saint-Tropez is located to Pampelonne Beach. The 2.8 mile (4.5km) long sandy beach between Cap Pinet in the north and Cap Camarat in the south is ranked as one of the most beautiful on the Côte d'Azur; one section is even called Plage Tahiti. Long stretches with sun-worshippers recumbent on their beach towels are interspersed

Mr T: "Electric scooters are a great complement to the Tesla. The little runabouts not only look cool, they also work really well."

with trendy beach bars and restaurants such as the Moorea and Club 55; the latter opened in 1955 and was the hangout for Vadim's film crew. At Pampelonne Beach you can go for long walks or paddle-boarding, take a diving course, or rent a kayak and simply row across the turquoise-colored seas.

to eat

In a small side street of Saint-Tropez's old town you'll find the traditional restaurant L'Auberge des Maures, opened in 1931. The menu includes Provençal cuisine featuring fish and seafood, with a fair-priced three-course meal. The Auberge also lives off the aura of the past—stars and artists such as David Niven and Pablo Picasso have signed the guestbook, and enthused about the cuisine, and Louis de Funès enjoyed the beef ragout here after shooting his "Gendarme" films.
L'Auberge des Maures
4 Rue Dr Boutin
www.aubergedesmaures.fr

BENELUX

MADE IN LOUISE

Brussels, Belgium

The Made in Louise, a family-run, small but elegant "home from home" in one of the most beautiful districts of Brussels, has certainly earned its reputation as a boutique hotel.

hotel info:

Made in Louise
Rue Veydt 40
B-1050 Bruxelles
Tel.: +32 2 5374033
Mail: info@
madeinlouise.com
Web: www.
madeinlouise.com

charging facilities:

1 Tesla DeC (Tesla only)
Garage for Model S max

Made in Louise, an endearing mix of bed and breakfast guesthouse and boutique hotel, is ideally located right in the heart of Ixelles, Brussels' famous Art Nouveau district. The charming townhouse features forty-eight bright rooms, and is distinguished by its thoughtful design, tasteful, contemporary furnishings, and high degree of individuality. And even though the property currently only has two underground parking spaces, it also has a Tesla Destination Charger. Made in Louise's hosts, Mélanie and Martin Dechateau, are sister and brother who run the hotel with their mother, an interior designer. Guests are instantly made to feel at home with a warm

Mr T: "The warm atmosphere at the Made in Louise makes you forget you're actually in a hotel. It's homelier than home!"

welcome at reception. The small, shaded interior courtyard is a great place to retreat and quietly reflect on the many sights and sounds experienced in the bustling European Quarter or the central Grand-Place. Another bonus is the large, all-day honesty bar that provides free coffee, tea, and homemade juice. An open fireplace and classic billiards table, meanwhile, set the perfect scene for seeing out the day in comfort.

AROUND BRUSSELS
Belgium

An intersection of cultures and symbol of European unity

Brussels is almost synonymous with the European Union. If this conjures up images of gray bureaucrats, you will be very surprised by the lively old town, the modern European Quarter, the city's culinary heritage and its beautiful surrounding countryside.

Grand-Place / Grote Markt
(approx. 2 miles/3km)

The beating heart of Brussels is the Grand-Place or Grote Markt (the Belgian capital is bilingual Walloon and Flemish). This is home to the magnificent Gothic town hall, whose façade is adorned with stately columns. Lining the square on all quarters are numerous guild houses forming a homogeneous body of buildings that has been classified as a UNESCO World Heritage Site since 1998. Every two years in August, the Grote Markt is transformed into a giant Flower Carpet measuring 230 x 66ft (70 x 20m) and making for a particularly striking vision from the balcony of the city hall. The square is always a great starting point for a stroll through the old town, with its picturesque lanes packed with bars and pubs.

Atomium
(approx. 6 miles/10km)

Measuring 334.6ft (102m) in height, the Atomium was once a symbol of the belief in progress; today, it is one of Brussels' main landmarks. The shimmering silver steel structure represents an iron crystal consisting of nine atoms, which has been enlarged 165 billion times. It was erected for Expo 58, the first world fair to be held after World War II. It's possible to explore the Atomium and spend some time in six of the

Mrs T: "A 20-minute walk will take you to the historic center of Brussels with its bars serving moules frites and Trappist beer."

spherical "atoms." A small exhibition provides information on the structure. One atom features a spectacular light installation, while the highest one houses a restaurant that provides a fantastic view of the convention facilities below, as well as the European Quarter, and in the distance, central Brussels.

to eat
Belgian waffles are a big temptation in Brussels, and there seem to be many who give in to this temptation—in any case, you can find waffle stalls at most street corners. The tasty treats are made of a soft dough, cooked in a waffle iron with a square grid and then "upgraded" with a variety of sweet treats: chocolate, strawberries, bananas, vanilla, cream, and... simply irresistible!

Belgian waffles at every street corner

THE PAND HOTEL

Bruges, Belgium

The Pand Hotel is a small gem in the heart of Bruges. Combining the charm of a historic mansion with the modern facilities visitors expect today, it is an ideal location for a city break.

hotel info:

The Pand Hotel
Pandreitje 16
B-8000 Bruges
Tel.: +32 50 340666
Mail: info@
pandhotel.com
Web: www.
pandhotel.com

charging facilities:

1 Tesla DeC (Tesla only)

The Pand Hotel is situated near Bruges' central marketplace. Manager Katelijne Haelters and her team warmly welcome their guests to this 18th-century burgher house, which has been converted into a modern luxury boutique hotel with a great sense of design and attention to detail. Precious antiques and original artworks are found throughout the property. With its wooden floor and paneled walls, the lounge has the feel of an English country manor house, while the open fire flickers gently in the reading corner of the lounge. All twenty-eight rooms and suites are individually appointed, combining classic style with modern comfort. Of particular note are the large, free-standing bathtubs and magnificent four-poster beds in the suites, whose windows often provide scenic views over the rooftops of Bruges. There is no breakfast buffet, but instead a menu filled with delicious treats that are then freshly prepared and served at your table. When the weather is mild, you can eat outside in the interior courtyard, and admire the little decorative fountain and the large clock on the wall.

> *Mr T: "Once again it is a pity that we have to continue on our journey. With more time, we would have liked to join the guided tour offered by the hotel."*

AROUND BRUGES
Belgium

The riches of the past and the sweet tastes of today

Bruges is one of Europe's best preserved cities. Picturesque cobbled lanes and peaceful canals link pretty market squares, historical churches, and elegant townhouses. Add beautiful shops, bars and, of course, chocolate and you have the perfect holiday destination.

Grote Markt (approx. ½ mile/1km)

Surrounded by *grachts* ("town canals"), the old town is home to the Grote Markt, the epicenter of Bruges. The square covers an area of around 2½ acres (1ha) and is bordered by the belfry on one side. Those fit enough can climb the 366 steps up the 272ft (83m) high and slightly crooked 13th-century bell tower, and will be rewarded with a fantastic view of the Grote Markt and the city. Soaring up among the many burgher houses lining the other side of the square is the Neo-Gothic courthouse with its slender spire. As the Grote Markt is largely car-free, the cafés, bars, and restaurants are very popular among locals and tourists alike—and, with a bit of luck, you might even be able to enjoy some festival performances around the statue of two local medieval Flemish patriots.

Chocolate Museum (approx. ½ mile/1km)

Bruges boasts a long chocolate-making tradition, and this is apparent not only in the numerous chocolate stores in the inner city, but also in the Choco-Story chocolate museum, where you'll learn all there is to know about the 5,500-year evolution from the original consumption of cocoa as a beverage to the present-day wonders of chocolate in its myriad forms and varieties, from bitter to sweet, in square blocks or round pralines.

Mrs T: "It's like a fairy tale. This lovely hotel has something of the feel of a luxuriously decorated dolls' house—in full size."

There are some 1,000 exhibits to explore, along with statues from Central America, where the Maya and Aztecs considered cocoa to be the "beverage of the gods." Or watch a live demonstration of chocolates being made by hand from select raw ingredients—then sample the results.

to eat

Near the hotel is the gourmet restaurant De Karmeliet. Owner and chef Geert van Hecke uses locally grown vegetables and fish from the nearby North Sea for his delicious meals, and has been the proud holder of an amazing three Michelin stars since 2006. The perfect wine to accompany your gourmet feast can be selected from the extensive wine list, which features 600 different wines and is inches thick!

De Karmeliet
Langestraat 19
B-8000 Brugge
www.dekarmeliet.be

QO AMSTERDAM
Amsterdam, The Netherlands

The QO Amsterdam is a wonderful hotel offering an energy-charged stay in the Netherlands' capital. The hotel cleverly combines design and innovation with sustainability.

Situated in Amsterdam's Ombal district, south of the old town, the QO Amsterdam may at first glance appear to be a 20th-century international-style office block, yet it quickly reveals itself as an innovative city hotel for the contemporary traveler. The modern, individually appointed rooms all boast floor-to-ceiling windows offering spectatcular views of the city. And the main theme that runs through the entire property is its multi-faceted approach to energy conservation and sustainability. In summer, for instance, the room temperatures are kept cool through the use of automatic blinds, while excess warmth is pumped into an aquifer-based heat storage

Mrs T: "Although the QO hotel is a vast complex, we never felt any sense of anonymity. It's a showcase hotel in terms of sustainability."

tank 230ft (70m) below ground, where it is stored until required for heating in winter. A greenhouse on the roof supplies vegetables for the hotel kitchen and provides shade for the under-cover open-air bar. In the kitchen, care is taken to ensure no food goes to waste—even breakfast is prepared to order, using local seasonal and organic products. Bikes are available for hire—the perfectly emission-free way to explore the city's attractions.

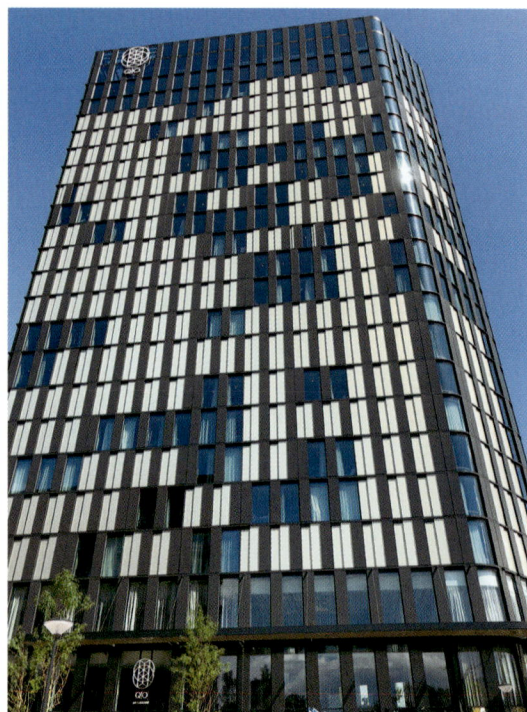

AROUND AMSTERDAM
The Netherlands

Canals, art, and coffee houses

Amsterdam is one of the liveliest capital cities in Europe as its canals, museums, architecture—and famous coffee houses—attract visitors from all over the world. But it is possible to find a quiet spot in its art galleries to sit and admire a Rembrandt, Van Gogh, or Vermeer.

Rijksmuseum
(approx. 3 miles/5km)

The Rijksmuseum is the largest building at the central Museumplein, Amsterdam's "museum square," and one of the Netherlands' national museums. The collections encompass artifacts on Dutch history and colonial history, along with Asian art. The Rijksmuseum is most famous, however, for its more than 2,000 paintings from the country's "golden age" in the 17th century. Among the most important exhibits are Rembrandt's *The Night Watch*, Jan Vermeer's *The Milkmaid*, Jacob van Ruisdael's *Landscape with Waterfall*, and Frans Hals' *The Merry Drinker*. The museum's research library, meanwhile, holds more than 160,000 titles, making it the largest library dedicated to the art history of the Netherlands.

Canal District
(approx. 3 miles/5km)

The Negen Straatjes ("nine streets") are hidden inside the canal belt: nine narrow lanes, packed with nice little individual shops and cafés. Here it is not the large chain stores that rule the roost; instead, shops selling second-hand clothes, records, and shoes as well as jewelry, art, purses, and natural cosmetics are lined up here. The shop owners all sell an individual product range, and each shop has its very own, personal style. In addition you will

Mr T: "Rigorously applied energy efficiencies and the well-integrated use of energy perfectly fit the concept of electric cars."

find lots of restaurants, cafés, and tearooms in the Nine Streets, where you can fortify yourself after having walked the first four streets and before setting out to do the other five. If you lose the overview from all the window-shopping, you can visit the National Museum of Spectacles to regain 20/20 vision.

to celebrate

For ten days in August every year, Amsterdam celebrates the Canal Festival. On offer is a wide range of classical and jazz, as well as music from other cultures. The entire city of Amsterdam becomes one giant festival venue, with a program of more than 250 concerts in 90 different locations. Grachtenfestival

www.grachtenfestival.nl

↑ Unmistakable: a street scene in Amsterdam, featuring its archetypal canals and countless bicycles.

ITALY

↑ High-quality, natural materials were used in the design of all the buildings and the garden, and everything blends harmoniously into the Tuscan countryside.

ADLER SPA RESORT THERMAE

Bagno Vignoni, Italy

The ADLER Spa Resort THERMAE, with its unique location in the Val d'Orcia, south of Siena, combined with the region's 2,000-year-old spa tradition, offers its guests total relaxation.

hotel info:

ADLER Spa Resort
THERMAE
Strada di Bagno
Vignoni 1
I-53027 San Quirico
Tel.: +39 0577 889000
Mail: info@adler-
thermae.com
Web: www.adler-
thermae.com

charging facilities:

1 Tesla DeC (Tesla only)
3 other DeC (all EVs)

Travertine is a type of limestone that has been used to build many villas, palaces, and churches in Tuscany and throughout Italy over the centuries—yet only very few buildings are likely to have been positioned in a former travertine quarry, such as the ADLER Spa Resort THERMAE, a special place for guests who want to find their way back to nature—and to their inner selves. This is also encouraged by the architecture of the terracotta-colored building in the style of a Tuscan villa with side wings. The panoramic windows bring the magic of the Val d'Orcia, which often serves as a film setting, into the house—including the sky above—since the roof above the restaurant, looking much like a rectangular piazza, can be rolled back. Travertine warm tones of wood and clean lines characterize the interior design of the shared spaces as well as 90 superior and family suites.

Mrs T: *"For wellbeing and relaxation, the ADLER Spa is simply one of the top addresses—you'll feel like a newborn in no time at all."*

A tradition of wellness and viticulture

The large garden with the thermal area can look back on some 2,000 years of wellness tradition in the Val d'Orcia—the nearby hot spring in Bagno Vignoni was popular among Etruscans and Romans for the treatment of skin and joint complaints. Today, some of its water flows into the pools of the hotel. The "Argilla" of the Adler Spa Resort Thermae—a healing clay steam bath—also goes back to the Etruscans. Fitness equipment, a Turkish bath and a Finnish sauna complete the wellness program on offer. For your well-being, the hotel also boasts exquisite cuisine and outstanding wines. Chef Gaetano Vaccaro has been creating Tuscan and Mediterranean delicacies for fifteen years, using local produce, such as olive oil and herbs from the hotel's own gardens, as well as meat from local Chianina cattle. In addition to matching wines from the large wine cellar, excellent bottles from the neighboring Tenuta Sanoner vineyard, organic since 2009, now appear on the hotel's extensive wine list.

↑ The Tesla also enjoys the views of the hilly Tuscan scenery—if only in the form of photographic wallpaper inside the garage.

↑ The resort's pool and spa wellness-scape leave nothing to be desired. The generously sized pools also follow the guiding principle of using natural design and using traditional materials.

Insight ADLER Spa Resort THERMAE

The focus is on relaxation at the ADLER Spa Resort THERMAE. There are numerous programs for wellness in the spa as well as medical applications on offer, including Ayurvedic treatments and analyses conducted by professionals. Mrs. T consults the Ayurvedic doctor and asks him to assess her pulse and blood pressure history. The experienced specialist diagnoses that her air energy has become out of balance and proposes walks, heat treatments, and a gentle oil massage as a therapy. Meanwhile, Mr. T enjoys a massage, and stays fit in the gym and by swimming in the hotel's fabulous pool.

Whether a formal dinner in the courtyard or the casual elegance of a traditional manor house—the Tuscan way of life is almost ↑ instantly reflected in the guests' well-being.

AROUND BAGNO VIGNONI
Italy

Tuscan dreamscapes in town and countryside

Tuscany has been a top tourist destination for centuries. No wonder—where else can you find beautiful landscapes, a Mediterranean climate, a deliciously healthy cuisine, great architectural monuments, and such a wealth of art?

to celebrate

The Palio di Siena, Italy's most famous horse race, takes place twice a year in Piazza del Campo, Siena's main medieval square. The Palio della Madonna di Provenzano is on July 2 and the Palio della Assunta on August 16.
Ten horses and bareback riders represent ten of the seventeen contrade, or city wards, and wear the rich colors associated with their district. The Piazzo del Campo is circumnavigated three times and both races last no longer than three minutes. The victorious ward receives a Palio and its citizens celebrate for days!

Palio di Siena
www.comune.siena.it/
La-Citta/Palio
on August 16 each year

Pienza
(approx. 9 miles/15km)

Pienza is considered the world's first "ideal city" inspired by Renaissance humanism. Aenaeas Silvius Piccolomini, the future Pope Pius II, was born in the town then known as Corsignano in 1405. In 1459, he redesigned it based on Renaissance Utopian ideals and renamed it after himself. Roads from all sides run to the Piazza Comunale, where four main buildings stand. Aside from the Palazzo Pubblico (the city hall), and the Palazzo Vescovile, where the future Pope Alexander VI of the Borgia family resided, there are the three-naved cathedral and the Palazzo Piccolomini, home to the family of Pius II. Pienza is so typical of the Italian Renaissance that, in 1968, Franco Zeffirelli used the piazza and the Palazzo Piccolomini as the setting for his *Romeo and Juliet*, and UNESCO listed the Old Town as a World Heritage site in 1996.

Val d'Orcia (approx. ½ mile/1km)

If you were to look for a "genuine" Tuscan valley without slipping into postcard clichés, then the Val d'Orcia would be one of the top spots. Crossed in ancient times by the Roman Via Cassia and in the Middle Ages by the Frankenweg pilgrimage trail, the valley was immortalized during the Renaissance by painters from Siena and added to the UNESCO World Heritage list in 2004. Today,

Mr T: "While our Tesla is recharging, Mrs T and I can go for a ride on the rental e-bikes, and enjoy the Tuscan sunshine."

the natural and cultural-historical beauty of Val d'Orcia can be experienced on foot or by bike directly from the hotel. Enjoy a guided tour including a stop for wine-tasting, or simply go for a drive along the cypress-lined panoramic road in the Val d'Orcia. Equally fascinating is a visit of Bagno Vignoni and a journey in the footsteps of Etruscan and Roman spa guests to San Quirico d'Orcia.

Siena
(approx. 31 miles/50km)

Siena, with a population of 53,000, is located an hour's drive north of the hotel. Its old town, considered one of the most beautiful in Italy, has been a UNESCO World Heritage site since 1995. Its heart is the vast Piazza del Campo, built in the early 14th century on the site of an ancient amphitheater. Also on the Piazza is the Gothic Palazzo Pubblico with its 335ft (102m) high tower. The cathedral, with its exterior of white and black marble, dates from the same period. The church's Romanesque origins are still recognizable in the interior. Numerous palazzi are scattered across the districts, or *contrade*, including the Palazzo Salimbeni, seat of the oldest bank in the world, the Banca Monte dei Paschi di Siena, founded in 1472.

Montalcino
(approx. 11 miles/18km)

Montalcino is a small medieval country town, just 30 minutes from the hotel. Wine connoisseurs will recognize the name from the Brunello di Montalcino, an excellent red wine made from the Sangiovese grape. The town was fought over by Florence and Siena, as is witnessed today by the imposing 14th-century *fortezza* (fortress) built by Siena, which dominates the cityscape. Also worth seeing are the *duomo* (cathedral), dedicated to San Salvatore with its Neoclassical façade, the Palazzo dei Priori with its dominant tower in the main square, the Piazza del Popolo, as well as the small art museum Museo Civico and Diocesano d'Arte Sacra.

Abbey of Sant'Antimo
(approx. 15½ miles/25km)

The beautiful Abbey of Sant'Antimo rises in the hilly landscape a few miles south of Montalcino. The Benedictine abbey dates from the 8th century and, according to legend, was founded by Charles the Great. The Carolingian Chapel, now used as the sacristy or vestry, dates back to this period and stands out from the rest of the Romanesque complex due to its beautiful frescoes. The abbey itself was built after an earthquake in 1118. Since the abbey's influence diminished

↑ Sometimes it gets rough at the horse race around the Campo in Siena, and spectators would do well to follow the spectacle from a safe distance, behind the barrier. The bareback riders take around 100 seconds to complete three laps around the piazza.

↑ Instead of a large open area, the Piazza delle Sorgenti in Bagno Vignoni features a basin with thermal water.

in the 13th century, the church was never completed, and the abbey itself was eventually abandoned in 1462. A small community of Premonstratensian Canons settled in the Abbey in 1979. Their Gregorian chants offer a mystical experience.

CASTELLO DI POTENTINO

Seggiano, Italy

Run by a British couple, Castello di Potentino is a "family castle," located near the beautiful hilltop town of Montalcino, the ideal place to relax and discover the castle, its history, and its on-site winery.

hotel info:

Castello di Potentino
Località Potentino, 3
I-58038 Seggiano (GR)
Tel.: +39 0564 950014
Mail: mail@
potentino.com
Web: www.
potentino.com

charging facilities:

1 Tesla DeC (Tesla only)
1 DeC (all EVs)

The words emblazoned on the sign at the gates to the Castello di Potentino warn you to "Beware of the dog!" However, castle guests are welcomed with open arms by sister and brother Charlotte Horton and Alexander Greene—and friendly dogs and cats! The property, which sits on top of a hill in Tuscany's wild south, has been very tastefully restored by the owners, who have turned it into a "21st-century castle." The past is fused with the present at the Castello. The eight guest rooms in the historic quarters, for instance, are furnished with period pieces, and antique prints and tapestries adorn the walls. At the Castello di Potentino, guests are

Mr T: "Together with our hosts we enjoy our meals in the kitchen: homemade food, garden salad, and their house wine—delicious!"

a part of their hosts' lives; you all sit and dine together in the kitchen, where you can listen to stories about the castle's past, and learn all about the on-site winery and Charlotte's award-winning organic wines, as well as about the chatelaine's small hat factory. Those preferring peace and tranquility can take a leisurely stroll through the castle grounds and admire the artworks, or enjoy some time in and around the private pool.

AROUND SEGGIANO
Italy

Tuscany—a different take

The south of Tuscany is calmer, quieter, and even more beautiful than its northern parts. Its beauty lies in its unspoilt landscape, with stunning views of the rich, fertile, and mostly wooded countryside and the picture postcard medieval villages nestling in the rolling hills.

Around Monte Amiata
(approx. 12½ miles/20km)

The Monte Amiata, 5,702ft (1,738m) high, is the most striking peak in south-eastern Tuscany. Its neat, conical shape testifies to its volcanic origin, although the last eruption took place more than 180,000 years ago. These days, energy from the hot springs is being harnassed, for example at the geothermal power station in Piancastagnaio. For a personal treat visit the Bagni San Filippo thermal spas. The small town not only boasts a spa and health resort complex; it is also a great place to walk to the Balena Bianca, or "white whale"—the name given by locals to a large limestone formation on a rock by the hot springs. Unfortunately, you can no longer climb the lime terraces and bathe in the pools, as the rock is now a natural heritage site.

Pitigliano
(approx. 37 miles/60km)

The entire region has been shaped by its volcanic past—evidenced not only by extinct volcanoes, but also by numerous plateaux of friable volcanic tufa that rise like blocks out of the ground. The plateaux were a popular choice to establish settlements, as the elevation made it easy to protect the towns against military attacks. The famous city of Orvieto in neighboring Umbria developed in this man-

Mrs T: "The attractive pool is complemented by chairs and sunbeds specially designed for the Castello di Potentino."

ner, and the little gem of Pitigliano clings just as picturesquely to the cliffs, high above the surrounding valleys. Enchanting narrow lanes criss-cross the perfectly preserved medieval old town, whose fortification walls repeatedly open up to provide sweeping views over the magical countryside.

to celebrate

Throughout the year, the Castello di Potentino organizes a series of concerts featuring well-known musicians and live performances in the charming intimate courtyard of the Castello, as well as a small number of exhibitions in the gallery. There is also a program of courses such as painting classes.

Castello di Potentini
www.potentino.com/
pages/concerts#feature-concerts

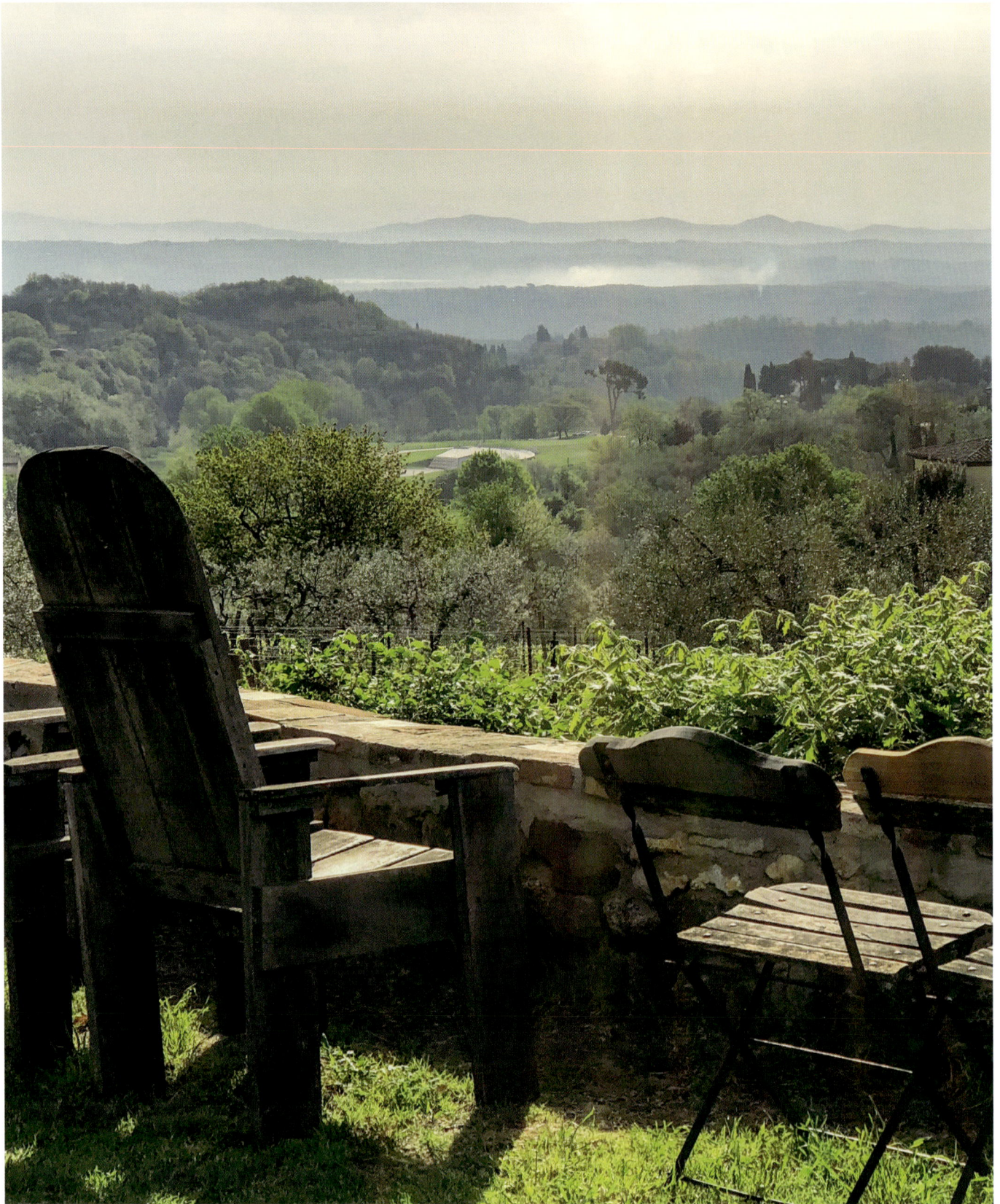

↑ There's a lot to see and explore in Tuscany, but those who spend the night at the Fattoria San Martino will be happy just to stay for a few days, to switch off and enjoy the views over the romantic countryside.

FATTORIA SAN MARTINO

Montepulciano, Italy

The family-run Fattoria San Martino in southern Tuscany is a sustainably renovated villa boasting a perfect garden where guests can leave their cares behind and escape into an Italian paradise.

hotel info:

Fattoria San Martino
Via di Martiena, 3
I-53045 Montepulciano
SI
Tel.: +39 0578 717463
Mail: info@
fattoriasanmartino.it
Web: www.
fattoriasanmartino.it

charging facilities:

2 Tesla DeC (Tesla only)
1 Tesla DeC (all EVs)

Not far from the historic winegrowing town of Montepulciano is a bed and breakfast guesthouse of a different kind: the Fattoria San Martino. Many years ago, owners Karin Lijftogt and Antonio Giorgini swapped the big-city congestion and noise of Milan for the vastness and tranquility of southern Tuscany, converting an old hillside villa and garden into a small but exquisite slow-life hideaway. Their dream of getting back to a simple rural lifestyle is exactly why the guesthouse has only three suites, one junior suite, and one family suite, whose names Mark, Flores, Miran, Sophia, and Casetta are quirkily endearing. The hosts place great emphasis on not being a "normal" hotel, but to bring their guests closer to nature. The couple treat all their guests as if they were old family friends ensuring their stay in this heavenly villa is as comfortable as possible. Karin, who is a former designer, individually planned all the rooms and suites, which are intentionally television-free, instead featuring specially crafted artworks or details, including cushions with slogans such as "Today is a good day."

Mrs T: "The Fattoria is hard to describe—you really have to experience the mixture of warmth and creativity for yourself."

A focus on sustainability

The Fattoria San Martino beautifully fuses luxury and sustainability, far from the crush and excess associated with mass tourism. Handyman Antonio made sure to only use natural materials when renovating the old villa. And in the garden, under the Tuscan sky, new solar panels stand in between the ancient olive trees, generating electricity for the Fattoria itself, as well as for the three Tesla Destination Chargers, which are elegantly integrated into the small parking lot. Much of the furniture at the property has been lovingly restored by Karin, including also the pieces for the small on-site restaurant, where she cooks dinner for her guests two or three times a week. In addition to homegrown and organic ingredients, her delicious vegetarian and vegan dishes sometimes include edible flowers from the garden. The herbal teas and organic wines served with the food are similarly sourced from the local area.

↑ The spacious suites of the Fattoria are friendly and all individually furnished.

AROUND MONTEPULCIANO
Italy

In the heart of the Tuscan hills

If you leave the cities of Pisa, Lucca, and Florence, with all their splendor and wealth of art treasures behind, you will discover an alternative Tuscany. Relax and enjoy the vine-covered hills, cypress-lined roads and gentle yellow fields of the region around Siena and Montepulciano.

Montepulciano (approx. 2 miles/3km)

On a hill only fifteen minutes' walk from the Fattoria is Montepulciano, which dates back to an Etruscan settlement from 8 BC and only narrowly escaped total destruction in World War II. The imposing Piazza Grande in the old town is home to the Renaissance Palazzo Comunale, whose tower provides superb views of the surrounding countryside, and the cathedral, from the same period, in whose plain bell tower is a large triptych that dominates the altar. Also on the square is the Pozzo dei Grifi dei Leoni ("the griffin and lion well'). A few lanes along, you could be forgiven for thinking you were in the midst of a *Commedia dell'arte* performance: an oversized mechanical figure of Pulcinella (Punch) from Italian folk theater strikes the hour on the Torre di Pulcinella at Piazza Michelozzo.

Drive to the south
(approx. 47 miles/75km)

Nothing is nicer than simply driving through the beautiful Tuscan countryside, especially if you take care not to pollute it with noise and unnecessary exhaust fumes by driving an EV. On your drive toward Pitigliano, you will reach the quieter southern parts of Tuscany and pass small towns and villages in scenic locations, always worth a detour—for example Abbazia San Salvatore, which is about half way. From almost anywhere, you will be

Mr T: "Enjoying your breakfast cappuccino on the terrace while overlooking the gently rolling hills of Tuscany—almost unbeatable!"

able to see the gently sloping Monte Amiata. Reaching a height of 5,702ft (1,738m), its uniform conical shape indicates its volcanic origin. Eventually, you will arrive at the enchanting medieval town of Pitigliano, nestled in the picturesque setting of a tufa plateau. As is customary in the south, it is very quiet here around noon, but then the streets get lively again in the evening.

Lago di Montepulciano
(approx. 9 miles/15km)

The Lake of Montepulciano is the centerpiece of the nature reserve of the same name, which was established in 1996 and covers an area of just under 2sq miles (5sq km). Located on

to drink

The Enoteca La Dolce Vita wine shop was established in an old town house in Montepulciano in 2005. Its range of wines comprises 600 different white and red wines from all regions of Italy, including the top wine from the local production area, the red "Vino Nobile di Montepulciano." The Enoteca also has a small restaurant, open daily from 12 noon to 9 p.m., where you can enjoy a glass with Tuscan specialties. And if you want to buy a bottle right away—it costs the same in the restaurant as in the store.

Enoteca La Dolce Vita Via di Voltaia Nel Corso, 80/82 www. enotecaladolcevita.it the border of neighboring province Umbria, the ¾ sq mile (1.9sq km) lake, whose average depth is 16½ ft (5m), is easily accessible by bike or as part of an extended hike. The La Cassetta visitors' center provides information on the area and its importance for migratory birds. It also presents historic artifacts from the fishing and agricultural industries that operated on and around the lake. To get a different perspective of the thick reed beds you can also take a trip onto the lake in a small solar-powered boat (in keeping with the electric vehicle theme) operating from the small jetty.

Chianciano Terme
(approx. 7½ miles/12km)

Located just a few miles south, Montepulciano's neighboring town of Chianciano Terme is not only home to a picturesque old town with historic buildings, such as the Collegiata di San Giovanni Battista Church and the Porta del Sole city gate, it is also a thermal spa town. The Etruscans, followed by the Romans, already knew that thermal springs could have health benefits. Today, five springs have been developed for treatment purposes. The modern spa complex was established in 1915, and expanded in the 1950s and 1960s. The Terme Sensoriali is a classic wellness center, while the Piscine Termali Theia thermal baths is famous for its large outdoor pool.

Torrita di Siena
(approx. 6¾ miles/11km)

The nearest town to the north is Torrita di Siena. First mentioned in 1037, from the 13th century onward Torrita fell under the influence of Siena. From this time, the castle and city walls, with the Porta Gavina and Porta a Pago gates, were used to safeguard Siena's rule, and did so successfully until 1554, when the city fell to Florence, which had in the meantime gained ascendency. Apart from its name, there is a very famous tradition that, since 1966, has paid tribute to Torrita's time under

↑ From the tower of the Palazzo Comunale on Montepulciano's Piazza Grande, the vista opens to the beautiful square with its cathedral and fountain, and also to the rolling hills of the surrounding countryside.

↑ Like many cities in Tuscany, Chianciano Terme is enthroned on a hill with wide views over the countryside. Warm springs already made the city a popular bath in ancient times.

Siena's control: the Palio dei Somari. Torrita di Siena's urban districts race one another in a similar fashion to the famous Palio di Siena, but only once a year in the second half of March, and on donkeys rather than horses!

↑ What a fantastic view! With the natural pool behind her, and the Tuscan countryside beyond, Mrs T is happily planning her itinerary for the next few days.

IL PALUFFO TUSCAN VILLA

Certaldo/Firenze, Italy

Nestled in a dreamy hillside setting in the heart of southern Tuscany, owner-managed il Paluffo Tuscan Villa uniquely combines history and sustainability to create a small but exquisite vacation paradise.

hotel info:

il Paluffo Tuscan Villa
Via Citerna, 144
I-50052 Certaldo FI
Tel.: +39 0571 664259
Mail:
info@paluffo.com
Web:
www.paluffo.com

charging facilities:

2 Tesla DeC (Tesla only)
1 Tesla DeC (all EVs)

Il Paluffo Tuscan Villa is nearly 600 years old; the oldest part of the heritage-listed complex—the olive mill—dates back to 1427. Newer sections, such as the main building, were added in the 17th century. Extensively and meticulously renovated, it is now a small bed and breakfast guesthouse located on a hill in the heart of Tuscany. There are four rooms with frescoed walls in the Manor House, as well as four self-contained apartments with kitchens in the Villa. The entire property exudes the warm hospitality of its hosts Liana and Luca. Liana is a descendant of the Paluffi family, after whom the guesthouse is named, and the couple aims to keep the property's history and traditions alive for future generations. They also place great emphasis on sustainability, and so they repaired and preserved the old flint mill, where olives were once pressed, as well as a giant clay trough, where grapes were pressed with bare feet. Today the couple is proud to be producing their organic olive oil and wine once more.

Mrs T: "Lying in a hammock by the pool, squinting into the sun, and inhaling the scent of wild herbs such as rosemary is my vision of heaven."

A sustainable holiday paradise

The owners are incredibly mindful of neutralizing il Paluffo's carbon footprint, and have continued their sustainability ethos by installing solar panels for hot water as well as a heat pump. They have also invested in a Tesla, which they use for their own emission-free journeys. This delightful holiday paradise offers many small luxuries to make their guests feel pampered and indulged. An iPad is provided in all rooms, allowing you to research your onward journey; and the large, natural pool is entirely chemical-free. The tranquil gardens surrounded by vineyards and olive trees are an oasis of peace; while the magnificent towers of San Gimignano are in the distance. Food is a topic close to every Italian's heart, and Liana and Luca are very accommodating in providing traditional Tuscan cooking lessons. The tastings of the house wines, however, are run by Liana herself, as a trained sommelier.

↑ The dignity of the entire building complex encourages guests to leave all their worries behind.

AROUND CERTALDO
Italy

The joy of life in lovely Tuscany

Whether you drive overland and capture the scents and sights of rural Tuscany, marvel at the medieval skyline of San Gimignano, wander through oak forests, or admire elegant Italians in a street café in fashionable Florence, the zest for life in the region is simply infectious.

Certaldo
(approx. 7½ miles/12km)

Certaldo is the name of the small town to which il Paluffo hotel belongs administratively; it can be reached in 15 minutes by car. From the new town by the river and the train line, you can either walk up the steep path to Certaldo Alto, the old town, or take the *funicolare*, a kind of cog railway. At the top you will find a tangle of lanes, picturesque houses, small cafés and restaurants, and a fabulous view over the Tuscan hills and the nearby towers of San Gimignano. You'll feel yourself transported centuries back in time. Don't miss the Palazzo Pretorio with its numerous coats of arms on the exterior façade and in the courtyard, and Boccaccio's House, the birthplace of the Renaissance author of the famous novella collection *The Decameron*.

Via Chiantigiana
(approx. 18½ miles/30km)

Nomen est omen ("the name is the sign") is a proverb coined by the ancient Romans, who practiced viticulture here some 2,000 years

ago, and Via Chiantigiana is what present-day Italians call the Strada Regionale 222, which winds its way through the Chianti wine-growing region. The roughly 47 mile (75km) road between Florence and Siena is one of the most beautiful routes in Tuscany, reached some 19 miles (30km) east of the hotel.

Mr T: "History meets state-of-the-art innovation at il Paluffo —a fine example of how the two can be sustainably combined!"

Numerous olive groves and vineyards line the road, punctuated by towering Mediterranean cypresses. Roughly halfway between those two ancient cities, you come across wineries such as Greve and Panzano in Chianti, which produce the world-famous Chianti Classico DOCG wine. Since many vineyards offer wine tastings along with a delicious snack, it is best to allow a whole day for traveling along the Via Chiantigiana.

San Gimignano
(approx. 14¼ miles/23km)

You can see the towers of San Gimignano from il Paluffo hotel, but it takes about half an hour to get there by car. It's worth it: The

to eat

One of Liana and Luca's favorite culinary spots is not far from il Paluffo: the Osteria di Casa Chianti. Here, excellent Tuscan cuisine based on old recipes including seasonal specialties and delicious wine are offered by a very extrovert owner who is ready to give you an unforgettable evening.

Osteria di Casa Chianti Between Fiano and Certaldo: Via delle Case Nuove 77 - Certaldo (FI) www.osteriadicasachianti.it

completely preserved medieval jewel, listed as a UNESCO World Heritage site, is unique because of its towers, which were built by the local patrician families trying to outdo each other at the time. If you don't suffer from vertigo, you can climb the towers to a height of about 164ft (50m) via narrow staircases and enjoy stunning views of the houses and the cathedral of San Gimignano as well as the Tuscan hills. Once you've come back down, the *gelato* at the Gelateria Dondoli will taste even better than you would expect of a place that has repeatedly been named the best ice-cream parlor in the world.

Berignone Forest Nature Reserve (approx. 34 miles/55km)

The Riserva Naturale Foresta di Berignone, located between Volterra and Pomarance is an ideal place for hiking. Mainly oak forest, the nature reserve extends approximately 5,000 acres (2,000ha) and is a home for numerous mammals, including wild boar and even wolves, as well as more than 50 species of birds. A number of signposted hiking trails run through the reserve, and information boards along the way tell you about the local flora and fauna. You'll also find the ruins of the medieval castles of Vescovi and Luppiano in the reserve, as well as several small rivers, including the crystal-clear Cecina near Masso delle Fanciulle, which is used for outdoor swimming in the summer.

Florence (approx. 23½ miles/38km)

Tuscany's capital city is one of the most popular tourist destinations and is easy to reach from il Paluffo. The largely car-free historic city center is home to the Cathedral of Santa Maria del Fiore with its imposing, brick-clad dome and the Uffizi Gallery, famous for its impressive collection of Renaissance art, including Botticelli's *The Birth of Venus* and Michelangelo's *David*—a copy of which stands outside. And what could be nicer than

↑ San Gimignano is called the "Manhattan of the Middle Ages" because of its many tall towers. Some are open to visitors, offering a magnificent view of the city and surrounding countryside.

↑ The breathtakingly beautiful scenery in Tuscany is also very varied, as here near Volterra.

strolling through the streets of the old town, shopping in one of the exclusive fashion boutiques, watching the street performers while sipping a delicious latte or prosecco, or visiting the jewelery and art shops on the Ponte Vecchio across the Arno River?

↑ The Piedmontese hill country with its fields, meadows, and vineyards is exceptionally fertile.

MARCHESI ALFIERI

San Martino Alfieri, Italy

The Marchesi Alfieri in Piedmont is a large winery with a historic castle and magical castle grounds that has been lovingly extended to include seven charming guest rooms.

hotel info:

Marchesi Alfieri
Piazza Alfieri, 28
I-14010 San Martino
Alfieri (AT)
Tel.: +39 0141 976015
Mail: info@
marchesialfieri.it
Web: www.
marchesialfieri.it

charging facilities:

2 Tesla DeC (Tesla only)
1 Tesla DeC (all EVs)

The Alfieri family from nearby Asti have spent many summers in the castle at the Marchesi Alfieri winery. Today, the castle and its winery are run by three sisters: Emanuela, Antonella, and Giovanna San Martino di San Germano. They have extended the complex to include a small bed and breakfast guesthouse called La Locanda. The guest rooms, found in several buildings throughout the sprawling complex, are furnished with antiquities from the family's own art collection. The hostesses ensure your breakfast is made from premium local produce—after all, wine has been made here since 1696. The good reputation of the winery also demands quality and

Mr T: "The castle park is a small forest, and truffles thrive in its fertile ground. At the right time, truffle dogs will sniff out the precious mushrooms."

sustainability in all the hotel's other activities. Something that will make your stay here extra special is the fact that guests are given the key to the castle grounds, which were laid out in the style of an English landscape garden in 1815. Here you can pick the perfect picnic spot under a Lebanon cedar or an ancient oak tree, open a bottle of wine from the hotel's vast cellars, and savor it alongside a zesty local cheese and delicious bread.

AROUND SAN MARTINO ALFIERI
Italy

Touring the vineyards of southern Piedmont

The Roman influence is still very evident in the archaeological treasures of the Piedmont region. Slow down and take the time to explore the region's history and enjoy the breathtaking beauty of its picturesque villages nestling amongst the verdant vineyards.

Alba (approx. 12½ miles/20km)

It is a half-hour scenic drive through the hills to the small town of Alba. Today, the town has a population of around 30,000, but in the Middle Ages, it was of great importance. Known as the "city of 100 towers," the structures were erected to represent the power of the noble families and to protect the city. Very few of them have survived, but the hallmarks of the once wealthy city linger on. Enjoy, for instance, a stroll through the alleyways, a visit of the stores, and a taste of delicious Piedmontese antipasti at the farmer's market—or other delicious dishes at one of the numerous restaurants. Be sure to try a glass of "Langhe," the delicious wine from the region around Alba. It is available as red, rosé, or white wine—the perfect partner for your meal.

Costigliole d'Asti and circuit (approx. 6¼ miles/10km, in total approx. 62 miles/100km)

Located just a few miles and a fifteen-minute drive away, the quaint town of Costigliole d'Asti is surrounded by vineyards. In clear weather, views from the hills extend as far as the Alps (below). In this typical wine-growing community you will find a handful of cafés and restaurants, where you can stop for a coffee or snack. Winegrowers also sell their own products, of course, most of which

Mrs T: "I wonder what the 300-year-old oak in the castle park has seen over time? Who has been kissed in its cool shade?!"

can be sampled before purchase. The full-day onward drive, includes stops in the picturesque historic villages of Neive, Serravalle Langhe, Monforte d'Alba, La Morra, Roddi, Guarene, and Priocca, taking in some stunning views of the scenery, before you return to the Castello dei Marchesi Alfieri.

to celebrate

In addition to the locally grown wines, the rare truffles are the second culinary specialty of the region. In Alba, the Fiera Internazionale del Tartufo Bianco d'Alba truffle fair takes place at the Palazzo Mostre e Congressi every fall. It is said to be the oldest white truffle fair, and is certainly one of the best known. The highlight of the event is the truffle auction, where traders buy not just in person, but also via satellite from around the world, at times paying astronomical sums for this delicacy.

Fiera Internazionale del Tartufo bianco
Alba
www.fieradeltartufo.org
October or November

RELAIS SAN MAURIZIO
Santo Stefano Belbo, Italy

The Relais San Maurizio is located on a gently sloping hill in the fertile region of Piedmont. As befits the name—Piedmont meaning "at the foot of the mountain"— numerous vineyards are spread out below the rolling hills.

hotel info:

Relais San Maurizio
Località San Maurizio, 39
I-12058 Santo Stefano Belbo (CN)
Tel.: +39 0141 841900
Mail: info@relaissanmaurizio.it
Web: www.relaissanmaurizio.it

charging facilities:

1 Tesla DeC (Tesla only)
1 Tesla DeC (all EVs)

The elegant Relais San Maurizio hotel lies a short drive south of Asti and is housed in a former monastery—reflected in the hotel's logo—that dates back to 1619. The sprawling complex has been recently restored and is now an upscale wellness resort. Its interior—with ceilings in many places revealing traces of the former monastery—and the ultra-stylish rooms offer a high level of comfort and luxury that is further enhanced by the exclusive spa facility. Relais San Maurizio has a large indoor pool, sauna, steam bath, a Kneipp water-treading pool, several rooms for beauty treatments and massages, a relaxation terrace, and even a must-see salt grotto.

> Mr T: "Here it's really easy to enhance all your senses—this is relaxation and rejuvenation at the very highest level."

Floating for twenty minutes in each of the two pools enriched with different types of mineral salts will leave you feeling amazingly energized and completely revived. The hotel is surrounded by a large and artistically landscaped garden which also includes an organic vegetable and medicinal herb garden, providing fresh ingredients for both the kitchen and the health treatments—just as it did when the monks lived here 400 years ago.

AROUND SANTO STEFANO BELBO
Italy

The land of truffles, wines, and good food

Where in Italy can you find the best food? Competing for the title of the world's most popular cuisine, Piedmont's prospects for first prize are excellent: a region blessed with wonderful wines, their famous black and white truffles, and many local specialties.

Asti (approx. 19 miles/30km)

Anyone traveling through the vineyards of southern Piedmont will want to make a detour to Asti. After all, who wouldn't associate that name with *spumante*, or "sparkling" wine? Now somewhat discredited as a mass-produced drink, there are some excellent alternatives, including Moscato d'Asti, an equally sweet sparkling wine that is superbly fruity and very light when produced well, and definitely worth trying as you while away the summer afternoon on the piazza. And when you're looking for a little adventure, take a stroll through the medieval old town with its individual shops and lovely cafés. Visit the Gothic cathedral with its much older crypt, admire the 13th-century city towers, or discover the birth house of poet and Enlightenment figure Vittorio Alfieri (1749–1804), an ancestor of the Marchesi Alfieri's owner (see page 90).

Barolo (approx. 27 miles/43km)

The name Barolo will be music to any serious wine lover's ears. And considering the worldwide acclaim of this winegrowing region, the town of only 700 residents is rather inconspicuous. It is, however, definitely worth the forty-five-minute drive from the hotel. Its medieval castle located up high on the hills cuts a majestic and imposing figure, and is home to a small museum and a historic library. The

Mrs T: "It's fab to be relaxing on the sun loungers by the outdoor pool while enjoying the panoramic views of the vineyards."

Enoteca Regionale del Barolo is situated in the cellar, where the focus is on promoting the region's famous wine. You can try the wines at a tasting session and if you like what you've tried can arrange wine delivery directly to your home. Or simply load any purchases into your Tesla trunk.

to eat

The excellent restaurant Guido da Costigliole offers typical Piedmontese cuisine with some modern touches. Respect for tradition and local ingredients is a key feature of the delicious dishes served here such as the highly recommended *agnolotti al plin*, the iconic Piedmontese pasta dish. To accompany the food, you have a choice of 3,000 wines, divided by region— Piedmont, France, and the rest of the world.

I-12058 Santo Stefano Belbo CN
Località San Maurizio
www.guidosanmaurizio.com/#ristorante

VILLA SPARINA RESORT
Monterotondo, Italy

The Villa Sparina Resort, located between Alessandria and Genoa, is highly recommended for nature and wine lovers who want to spend time in southern Piedmont, relaxing and enjoying good food.

hotel info:

Villa Sparina Resort
Frazione
Monterotondo, 56
I-15066 Gavi (AL)
Tel.: +39 0143 607801
Mail: info@
villasparinaresort.it
Web: www.
villasparinaresort.it

charging facilities:

2 Tesla DeC (Tesla only)
1 DeC (all EVs)

The winding roads of Piedmont snake through the vineyards of Monterotondo, before finally reaching the iron gates of the Villa Sparina Resort and its large interior courtyard. The resort is housed in a traditional, extensively restored winery, and its charming host, Alfonso Spinelli, is only too happy to take you on a tour of the hotel (L'Ostelliere) in the tranquil complex. The hotel's thirty-three rooms are spacious and tastefully appointed with a dash of vintage chic. Earthy colors create a warm and cozy atmosphere, enhanced by the ivy framing the windows adding a romantic touch. The former hen house in the lovely, expansive garden

Mr T: "Recharge your own batteries at the Villa Sparina! We loved the local Monterotondo wine served here."

is today the hotel's restaurant, fittingly called *La Gallina* ("The Hen"). The menu features all the gastronomic classics the Piedmont region is famous for. The flavorsome dishes are perfectly matched by the house wines from the hotel's own giant wine cellar. Villa Sparina's standout wine is the white Monterotondo in its specially designed bottle. You can enjoy superb views of the surrounding countryside from the restaurant.

AROUND MONTEROTONDO
Italy

Between Piedmont and Liguria

Where the two Italian regions meet, their respective traditions combine beautifully. A journey from urban Alessandria to the old port city of Genoa reveals a wide diversity ranging from the rural simplicity in an agricultural area via small industrial enterprises to the cosmopolitan hub of the busy metropolis.

Alessandria (approx. 20 miles/33km)

Alessandria, the provincial capital, is situated half an hour's drive from the hotel, on the banks of the Tanaro River in the Po Valley. As you stroll through the old town between the Public Gardens by the train station and the Piazza Matteotti with its triumphal arch, it is worth visiting two establishments in particular: the Borsalino Hat Museum and the Soave Art Gallery. The museum is devoted to the famous Borsalino (felt) hat, as well as top hats and other headwear made by the Borsalino brothers in the old factory building. The Soave Art Gallery, meanwhile, exhibits modern and contemporary art in a former church. Leaving the historic center behind and crossing the Tanaro, you will reach the giant Baroque citadel with its star-shaped bastions.

Genoa (approx. 32 miles/52km)

The Villa Sparina Resort is near Piedmont's border with Liguria, and also only a seventy-five-minute drive along the winding SP160 through the Apennine Mountains to the port city of Genoa. For centuries, the Republic of Genoa was a successful maritime trading state, and is also the birthplace of Christopher Columbus, the famous navigator. Parts of the old town, with its historic palaces, were named a UNESCO World Heritage Site in 2006, and have since been largely restored. In the central

Mrs T: "In fine weather one of my greatest pleasures is enjoying the view of the vineyard from one of the swings in the garden."

Piazza de Ferrari are the Palazzo Ducale and the Carlo Felice opera house. Down by the Ligurian Sea, the new aquarium—the largest in Europe—is surrounded by cafés and restaurants, the perfect places to watch the comings and goings at the Old Port, which was given a facelift for the Genoa Expo in 1992.

RELAIS SAN LORENZO
Bergamo, Italy

The Relais San Lorenzo is an exquisite boutique hotel situated on the edge of the old town of Bergamo Alta, which, in addition to the quality of its rooms, also wows guests with its superb cuisine.

After driving through the narrow lanes of Bergamo's Città Alta, you will reach the Relais San Lorenzo, where a friendly porter will immediately take your luggage to your room, while one of his colleagues hooks the Tesla up to the Destination Charger in the garage. The hotel has been tastefully renovated—clean lines and the classics of Italian design with a modern touch are the dominant theme in the rooms and suites, some of which have a free-standing bathtub. Be sure to also visit the spa facilities, where you can relax in the steam bath and the Finnish sauna, or indulge with massages and beauty treatments—the large Jacuzzi on the terrace provides fantastic views. The hotel also has your culinary needs covered. The Hostaria Gourmet Restaurant, which has been integrated into an archaeological excavation site, serves exquisite Italian meals made from local and seasonal ingredients—similar to the Hostaria Bistro, which offers more traditional fare. And when it comes to treating yourself to a drink, simply head to Relais San Lorenzo's terrace by day, or the lounge bar by night.

> *Mrs T:* "*My personal highlight: the free-standing bathtub and a separate shower fitted with chromotherapy. The most amazing bubble bath ever!*"

AROUND BERGAMO
Italy

A city on two planes

Two funicular railways connect Bergamo's old town—built high in the foothills of the Alps—with the lower-lying districts, some of which extend down to the Po Valley. The historic Città Alta is a listed heritage site. For culinary treats, try down-to-earth polenta and Taleggio cheese, two Bergamo classics, in one of the many excellent restaurants!

Città Alta
(approx. ½ mile/1km)

Bergamo's historic center and upper town, known as Città Alta (Upper City), was built on top of a heavily fortified hill, which is also accessible via a small funicular railway. Winding lanes, the cathedral, the churches, and the many city palaces make this center a true architectural treasure trove. There is an overwhelming array of cozy cafés, bars, and restaurants, guaranteeing a lively atmosphere on the central Piazza Vecchia, with the Palazzo della Ragione and a fountain circled by lion statues. A small museum is dedicated to Bergamo's most famous son, the opera composer Gaetano Donizetti and directly opposite the Relais San Lorenzo are the natural history museum and the archaeological museum.

Lago d'Iseo (approx. 23 miles/37km)

Lago d'Iseo or Lake Iseo, one of the most beautiful lakes in northern Italy, is about a half-hour drive from the hotel. Surrounded by high mountains, the lake is best explored in a clockwise direction from Sarnico. This will enable you to pull over by the roadside at any time and take photographs of the spectacular panoramic vistas as they unfold. You will have a lovely view of the little Island of San Paolo on your right as you emerge from the tunnel between Predore and Gallinarga. In

Mr T: "From the Relais San Lorenzo it is only a stone's throw to the heart of Città Alta. With its squares and lanes it's reminiscent of Rome."

2016, the artist Christo created a pedestrian access to this island from the southern shores of the larger Monte Island, using orange pontoons as part of his temporary *The Floating Piers* installation. Toward the end of the drive, Iseo's scenic lakeside promenade is the ideal place for a walk and cappuccino.

to celebrate

The Bergamo Jazz Festival has now secured a permanent place in the calendar of jazz enthusiasts from all over the world, along with the great international festivals at Paris, New York, Berlin, and Montreux. At Bergamo, Italian musicians alternate with international jazz greats. The venues are equally thrilling, as the concerts are performed on historical sites and places around the city where you would least expect them.
Bergamo Jazz Festival www.facebook.com/ bergamojazzfestival/ March

LIDO PALACE
Riva del Garda, Italy

The Lido Palace in Riva del Garda is a five-star hotel where history meets design—old and new form a perfect symbiosis that makes the hotel an unforgettable Italian holiday destination.

At the far northern end of Lake Garda, where the roads snaking around the mountains get ever windier and the views ever more spectacular, a stunning Art-Nouveau mansion stands on perfectly landscaped gardens, just east of the center of Riva del Garda: the Lido Palace. Originally opened in 1899, the hotel was exquisitely renovated by Italian star architect Alberto Cecchetto several years ago. His use of glass in the avant-garde extension and the giant windows on the new fifth floor provide sensational lake views, while the interior is modern, accentuated with high-quality fabrics and stylish décor. And although the Lido Palace has only forty-two rooms, hotel

Mr T: *"The hotel reflects the enchanting countryside around Riva: imposing limestone cliffs and lush vegetation, mirrored in the waters of the lake."*

manager Gabriele Galieni and his team offer the same perfect service you would expect at a large luxury resort. You can also experience this exemplary hospitality when visiting the large wellness facility in the basement or Il Redella Busa restaurant, located on the first floor of the sleek extension overlooking Lake Garda. The specialties created by head chef Giuseppe Sestito are a mouth-watering feast for all gourmets.

↑ If the weather is fine, guests can enjoy the superb panorama of the mountains and the lakes from the terrace.

AROUND RIVA DEL GARDA
Italy

Picture book Italy by Lake Garda

A Mediterranean climate in an Alpine panorama—this idyll on the northern Italian lakes, especially Lake Garda, has fascinated tourists for hundreds of years. Yet, amid all the hustle and bustle, you can still find ways to enjoy the serene beauty of the landscape and the untouched Italian way of life.

Rocca (approx. 547yds/½km)

After just a short walk toward the historic center of Riva, you come face to face with the impressive Rocca, the moated castle complex on the shores of Lake Garda. Originally built in 1124, the complex acquired its present-day appearance in the 19th century under the Habsburgs, who used it as a barracks. On the inside walls, fragments of elaborately restored Renaissance frescoes attest to even earlier times. These days, the Rocca is home not to Austrian soldiers, but to the MAG, the Museo Alto Garda. In addition to the history of the city and the nearby Sarca Valley, and an archaeological collection, the MAG also exhibits works of art in its gallery, predominantly 19th-century landscape paintings.

Busatte-Tempesta Panoramic Hiking Trail on Lake Garda (approx. 3 miles/5km)

Busatte, above Riva's neighboring municipality of Torbole, is barely a ten-minute drive from the hotel. The parking lot of a small adventure park marks the start of the panoramic hiking trail to Tempesta further south.

The entire trail runs 328–656ft (100–120m) above Lake Garda, offering spectacular views of the lakeside towns, sailboats, surfers, ferries, and the mountains in the west. The trail is suitable for beginners, as it has minimal climbs and descents, and even these are

Mrs T: "Architecture and interior design—everything fits together perfectly. We must admit: the Italians have plenty of style."

mostly in the form of steps with railings. The return trip is approximately 6¾ mile (11km) long. If you wish, you can follow part of the route to Tempesta on a well-defined forest path situated somewhat higher than the actual panoramic trail, or simply take a bus back to Torbole from Tempesta.

↑ The Naturhotel Rainer is located at almost 3,280ft (1,000m) altitude. In summer you can relax on the beautiful outdoor terrace, while in winter, skiing and sauna are the top activity choices for guests.

NATURHOTEL RAINER

Racines, Italy

For 40 years, the Naturhotel Rainer in the South Tyrolean mountains has been a destination for hikers and other nature-loving guests who are looking for relaxation and rejuvenation.

hotel info:

Naturhotel Rainer
Jaufental/Mittertal 48
I-39040 Ratschings
Tel.: +39 0472 765355
Mail: info@
hotel-rainer.it
Web: www.
hotel-rainer.it

charging facilities:

1 DeC (all EVs)
2 CEE 16A
3-phase (all EVs)

The family-run Naturhotel Rainer is located in the quiet Jaufen Valley in Racines, less than fifteen minutes from Vipiteno and the Italian Brenner highway. Proprietor Hannes Rainer, his wife Kathrin, a certified fitness trainer, and sister Sabrina, who takes care of the interior decorating, continue the family traditions established by their father, hotel owner and hiking guide, Hans Rainer and his wife, Marialuise who created the hotel in 1979, next to the existing farm and inn. A "wellness" hotel, the modern Tyrolean idyll is utterly committed to sustainability. Local

Mr T: "*The saltwater swimming pool impressively shows that it's possible to dispense with any chemical additives, such as chlorine.*"

↑ The road to the hotel in the Jaufen Valley runs right through the small chapel, which was simply cut in half.

pine and larch wood, for example, dominate the interiors in the bright rooms and suites. The 517sq ft (48sq m) Eagle's Nest Suite is particularly impressive. Its panoramic southwesterly windows open up to superb views across the Jaufen Valley while comfortably seated on the Eagle's Nest Swing. The luxurious cushions are filled with hay from the hotel's own Ontrattalm alpine pasture.

A special trilogy

The Naturhotel Rainer promises its guests the threefold attractions of hiking adventures in the South Tyrol, delicious, light cuisine, and a range of spa treatments using natural local products. There are at least three guided hikes every week, including one with hotel owner Hans Rainer, to the hotel's alpine meadow, the Ontrattalm, where he lights the barbecue for his guests. His son, Hannes Rainer, is a gourmet chef and ensures that only seasonal and regional natural products are used in the kitchen and then flavored with herbs from the hotel's own herb garden and surrounding alpine meadows. Hans' daughter-in-law, Kathrin Rainer, for her part, guarantees that the hotel's small Naturbadl spa and beauty center on the Bergbach adjacent to the hotel only uses products that are free from chemicals and preservatives, and instead full of South Tyrolean ingredients, such as mountain honey, mountain arnica, and St. John's wort. Living in harmony with nature ensures Naturhotel offers guests total mental and physical rejuvenation.

↑ Wood and other natural materials predominant in the Naturhotel Rainer, where nature and sustainability are the cornerstone of the Rainer family's philosophy.

Insight Naturhotel Rainer

The Naturhotel Rainer is a family business in the best sense of the word. The Rainers have been running a hotel here since 1934, and the current senior manager, Hans Rainer, took over in 1978. His son, Hannes, is the next one in line. "I find my inner peace in nature," Hans Rainer says, and the hotel team do everything to ensure that guests can share that same experience. As such, the wellness area, for which junior manager Kathrin is co-responsible, and the excellent restaurant, run by hotel manager Hannes, both use natural and regional products whenever possible.

Large windows flood the rooms with light throughout the year. ↑
The food is equally heart-warming, featuring sophisticated cuisine using regional ingredients.

AROUND RACINES
Italy

South Tyrolean alpine bliss in the Jaufen Valley

Vipiteno (Sterzing) lies just a short drive from the Brenner Pass and from there it is only a few miles to Racines (Ratschings). You are now in the middle of the most beautiful South Tyrolean mountains with fantastic hiking and many superb castles, old churches, and gorges.

Jaufen Valley
(approx. ½ mile/1km)

The Jaufen Valley, where the hotel is located, is over 21.8 miles (35km) in length. It extends from the district of Gasteig to the 6,870ft (2,094m) high Jaufen Pass and is considered the quietest of the three valleys in the Racines municipality, making it ideal for relaxed rambling from spring to fall. The Jaufenhaus at 6,191ft (1,887m) altitude, dominated by Jaufenspitz and Saxner, is reached via hiking trail no. 12. Alpine pastures and huts, such as the Rinneralm, the Saxnerhütte, and the Kalcheralm, are popular hiking destinations, inviting you to relax in the beautiful scenery at the end of your tour. You can also try the hotel's early morning guided "Wellbeing Hikes" of about one hour, which include breathing exercises and herb picking.

Vipiteno (Sterzing)
(approx. 4½ miles/7km)

Vipiteno, the nearest larger town, is less than 15 minutes' drive away, and has always been an important transportation hub on the way to the Brenner Pass. The landmark of this picturesque old town is the tall twelve-turret tower from the late 15th century, which has a mechanical clock tower and a sundial. The parish church, Our Lady in the Moss, is also worth visiting. Outwardly still a late Gothic hall church, the interior was redesigned in the Baroque style. It's very pleasant simply

Mrs T: "This Naturhotel has its own Tesla, which guests can rent for days out and which is charged with hydroelectric power."

to stroll through the lanes of the old town. In the past, craftsmen had their workshops here; today you'll find for example shops selling traditional costumes, shoes, and regional specialties. The latter can, of course, also be sampled in the many restaurants and cafés.

Wolfsthurn Castle
(approx. 6¼ miles miles/10km)

Schloss Wolfsthurn, in Racines' Mareit district, is the only Baroque castle in the South Tyrol. Dating back to a medieval fortified tower, it was given its present look under Franz Andreas von Sternbach in the years 1727 to 1741. The eastern three-level main wing of the complex is connected to the single-floor

to celebrate

If you think of the Tyrol, dumplings come to mind. The Sterzing Dumpling Festival, which takes place every year in September, is dedicated to this ball-shaped culinary landmark. Spinach dumplings, bacon dumplings, cheese dumplings (known as Kasnocken) and sweet dumplings with apricot or plum fillings are served at a 1,312ft (400m) long table in Sterzing's Old Town.

Dumpling Festival, Sterzing Old Town www.knoedelfest-sterzing.com September

west wing via a large walled courtyard with a fountain. A number of state rooms in the main wing with Baroque exhibits can be visited, and a small exhibition explains the history of the building, in which the South Tyrolean Museum of Hunting and Fishing has also been housed since 1996.

Gilfenklamm (Gola di Stanghe) (approx. 3 miles/5km)

The Gilfen Gorge natural monument has been a popular destination for a one-hour hike since it was first discovered in 1898 and named Emperor Franz Joseph Gorge. Just a few minutes' drive from the hotel, the Ratschinger Bach near Weiler Stange is the only watercourse in Europe to have cut its way through a layer of white marble, which now looks green and gray due to weathering. From the boardwalk through the gorge with its numerous bridges you can admire the force of nature in the rushing torrent deep below. The water from the Stubai Alps and the area around the Jaufen Pass flows into the Ridnauner Bach, a tributary of the Eisack.

Merano (approx. 25 miles/40km)

If you drive over the Jaufen Pass, you'll reach Merano after about half an hour. Recognized as a popular health resort since the 19th century, one of the most famous guests at the spa was the Empress Elisabeth of Austria (popularly known as Sisi); there is even a monument to her. If you stroll along the small Passer River, you'll notice further sculptures and Mediterranean plants, which flourish in the mild climate of the town, situated less than 1,000ft (300m) above sea level. The new Merano Thermal Baths, built by Matteo Thun and opened in 2005, are situated in the large path along the Passer River. A highlight on the outskirts of the town is Trauttmansdorff Castle. The complex, remodeled in the neo-Gothic style from 1847, was the residence

↑ You can explore the Gilfenklamm via a circular route in about 2½ hours and combine the walk with a visit to the ruins of Reifenegg Castle. A small visitors' fee is payable at the entrance to the gorge.

↑ There are more than 80 awe-inspiring botanical garden landscapes at Trauttmansdorff Castle with magnificent mosses, trees and shrubs from around the world. A visit to the exotic Palm Café on the banks of the Water Lily Pond is the perfect ending to your trip.

of Empress Elisabeth during her spa stays. It now houses the Touriseum, the South Tyrol Museum of Tourism. However, the main focus is on the castle's beautiful, extensive botanical garden.

SWITZERLAND & LIECHTENSTEIN

CASTELLO DEL SOLE

Ascona, Switzerland

The Castello del Sole resort, located on a unique, scenic piece of land on Lake Maggiore in Ascona, offers five-star luxury for its guests, many of whom have become regulars.

hotel info:

Castello del Sole
Via Muraccio 142
CH-6612 Ascona
Tel.: +41 91 7910202
Mail: info@
castellodelsole.com
Web: www.
castellodelsole.com

charging facilities:

2 Tesla DeC (Tesla only)
1 Tesla DeC (all EVs)

The approach up the long driveway to the magnificent Castello del Sole in Ascona is a truly exhilarating experience. Once you arrive at the five-star hotel on the northern shores of Lago Maggiore, you will be personally welcomed by hotel manager Simon Valentin Jenni. The rooms and suites exude a dignified elegance that creates a real sense of the property's more than 110 year tradition. Of particular note is the stunning view of the 247 acre (100ha) Garden of Eden from the bungalow-style Retreat Loggia Suites. Apples and other agricultural products are grown here, but there are also numerous flowers, blossoming shrubs, hidden nooks for reading, comfortable deck chairs, and even a

Mr T: "Here you will find plenty of space, luxury, warmth, sun, delicious food, and a welcoming family environment."

private beach providing direct access to the lake. A love of nature and attention to detail are apparent throughout, be it in the beautiful floral arrangements that you find all over the property, the large luxurious spa facility, or the fantastic dishes made from home-grown ingredients and served at the Locanda Barbarossa restaurant. It is easy to see why Mattias Roock, the young chef de cuisine, has already been awarded a Michelin star and seventeen Gault-Millau points.

AROUND ASCONA
Switzerland

Swiss reliability
and the spirit of Italy

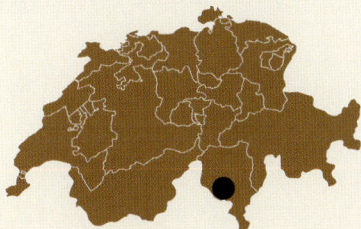

Lake Maggiore, perhaps the most beautiful of the northern Italian lakes, is shared by Italy and Switzerland. Here, in the north, the best of two worlds combine to create an almost unreal dreamscape of mountains, water, and urbane Mediterranean flair.

Ghisla Art Collection, Locarno
(approx. 2 miles/3km)

The three-story, russet-colored cube of the Ghisla Art Collection (below) cuts a striking figure on the inland lane of the road following the shores of Lago Maggiore in Locarno. Small but sophisticated, the gallery dates back to the private collection of Pierino and Martine Ghisla (curated for more than thirty years), its eight rooms showing masterpieces of modern and contemporary art, from Pop Art and conceptual art, to Informalist and abstract art, to New Dada. In addition to household names, such as Victor Vasarely and Joan Miró, the collection also features young, up-and-coming artists. The permanent exhibition is complemented by a number of temporary exhibitions every year, held on the cube's top floor.

Valle Verzasca (approx. 5 miles/8km)

The Verzasca is one of several mountain rivers that feeds into Lake Maggiore. Its valley, extending northward to the east of Locarno, is considered one of the most beautiful in the Ticino. It is very popular with hikers, and also makes for an exciting, environmentally friendly drive in your Tesla. As you hike or make regular stops along the way, you will see the Verzasca snaking its way among chestnut trees and broadening out into small natural basins, where its crystal-clear water shimmers

Mrs T: "This is paradise! The Castello del Sole has taken our hearts and minds by storm— all in just two days."

as if in a pool. The tracks in the lower section of the Valle Verzasca along the Lago di Vogorno dam, or around the mountain village of Lavertezzo, with its impressive Ponte dei Salti natural stone bridge, are easily accessible, while the higher parts of the valley are recommended for more experienced trekkers.

to celebrate

"And action!" Is the motto of the Locarno Festival every year in August. Many of the movies are shown in the open air on the central Piazza Grande, which can accommodate 8,000 spectators. Since 1988, it has awarded a top prize, the "Golden Leopard," with the prize money split between the director and the producer of the winning movie.

Locarno Film Festival
www.locarnofestival.ch
August

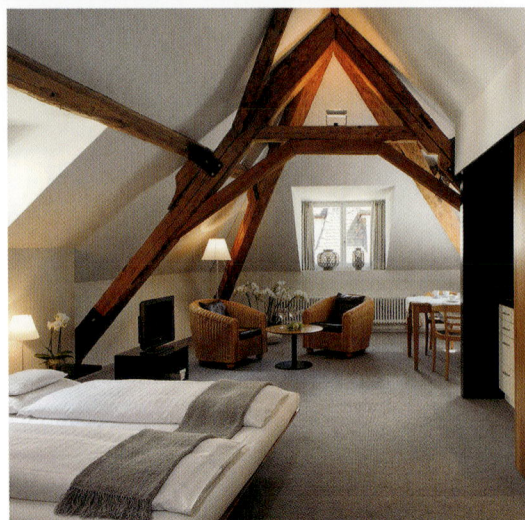

↑ The main building, constructed in 1834, blends harmoniously into the historic spa district of Baden. The film *Justice* (1993), based on Friedrich Dürrenmatt's novel, was shot here.

LIMMATHOF BADEN HOTEL & SPA

Baden, Switzerland

Switzerland's most mineral-rich thermal springs can be enjoyed
at the Limmathof Baden Hotel & Spa, whose two buildings are connected
to an impressive spa complex via a bridge across the river.

hotel info:

Limmathof Baden
Hotel & Spa
Limmatpromenade 28
CH-5400 Baden
Tel.: +41 56 200 17 17
Mail:
info@limmathof.ch
Web:
www.limmathof.ch

charging facilities:

1 Tesla DeC (Tesla only)
1 Tesla DeC (all EVs)

The Limmathof Baden is a hotel and spa consisting of two buildings: the stately, traditional Limmathof Baden Hotel & Novum Spa in the historic spa district of the city and—connected via a small bridge over the Limmat River—the ultra-modern, cube-shaped Limmathof Baden Hotel & Private Spa in the neighboring village of Ennetbaden. If you want to recharge your Tesla on a destination charger, make sure you head to Ennetbaden—you can walk there from Baden, and if you have a room in the "old building," it's just across the bridge. The historic building, completed in 1834, has an impressive neo-baroque dining room that served as a movie set in 1993. The hotel's tastefully furnished rooms, suites, and studios—harmonious, soft colors, rich woods, and natural stone—provide the perfect conditions for a relaxing stay and the healing waters of the thermal springs, 97°F (36°C), are the main focus at the Novum Spa. A visit to the gym at the Limmathof Baden Hotel & Novum Spa provides recreation and relaxation in a luxurious setting.

Mr T: "*The Limmathof believed in the future of electromobility right from the early days and so they installed two destination chargers.*"

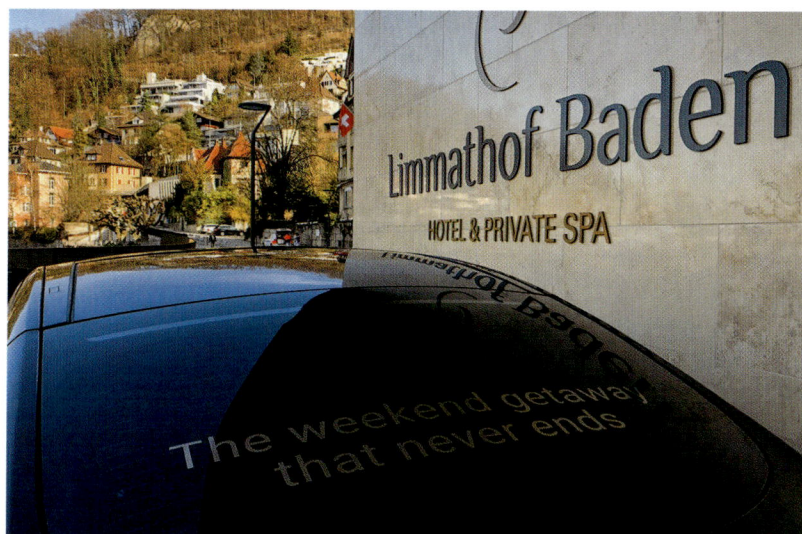

↑ Sustainability is part of the guiding concept for this traditional Swiss hotel, based in Baden and Ennetbaden.

Health, well-being, and sustainability

The Limmathof's commitment to its guests' comfort continues in their cutting-edge new building on the other side of the river, which opened in 2011. The Diamant, Saphir, and Rubin private spa suites there offer pampering and privacy in a monument to modernity, and the director, Lorenz Diebold, ensures you fulfill all your wellness needs and wishes. In the morning, as you wake up to the gentle gurgling sound of the Limmat River and the cheerful twittering of birds, or as you take a delicious breakfast at the in-house Café Bistro Hirsch, you'll find the "well-being" philosophy of the Limmathof Baden hotel complex clearly in evidence. The fact that your Tesla can recharge its batteries at the Limmathof is just as much a part of the Limmathof's sustainability concept as the idea of using the hot thermal waters not only to energize the hotel's bathers and spa guests, but also as the main source of heating for the complex.

AROUND BADEN
Switzerland

Where the Romans used to bathe

The Limmat meanders through the rocks at the meeting point of two geological zones— the Swiss Central Plateau and the Jura range. In the spa town of Baden, 21 thermal springs rise on both sides of the river. Their mineral-rich, pleasantly temperate waters have been used in spa cures for 2,000 years.

to eat

A sweet treat with history are the Spanish Brötli, which traditionally come from the Baden region. Shortly after it was introduced to Switzerland in the 18th century, this buttery puff pastry became so popular that wealthy Zurich residents also wanted to eat it for Sunday breakfast. However, since baking was not allowed on Sundays in the Reformation city, the gentle folk sent their servants by train to Baden to buy them. Consequently, the train route became known in the vernacular as Spanish-Brötli-Bahn. Today, the pastry is fêted every 10 years with the Badenfahrt—a major festival in Baden, which attracts more than 1 million visitors.

Museum Langmatt
(approx. ½ mile/1km)

Museum Langmatt, open from early March to early December, is located close to the hotel, and housed in the former villa of an industrialist family, Sidney William Brown and Jenny Brown-Sulzer. The Browns acquired their first two pictures on their honeymoon in Paris in 1896. From 1908, these art collectors concentrated on the French Impressionists: Paul Gauguin, Pierre-Auguste Renoir, Claude Monet, Alfred Sisley, and Paul Cézanne are just some of the painters, whose works are exhibited at the Museum Langmatt. The villa itself, built between 1899 and 1901, and its original furnishings, are also well worth seeing. The villa regularly hosts temporary exhibitions and the romantic park invites you to enjoy a picnic.

Grand Casino
(approx. ½ mile/1km)

More than 300,000 visitors a year come to the Casino to hear the commands, "Faites vos jeux!" and "Rien ne va plus!" The Grand Casino Baden, based in the former Kursaal dating from 1875, is open every day, and table games are possible from 3 p.m. In addition to classic games, such as roulette, blackjack, and poker, you can also play Big Shot, Black James, and Race4Ace at the casino. Regular events, including poker tournaments or bingo nights, as well as after-work parties with live

Mrs T: "Although I grew up here, the renovated Limmathof and the new spa were a huge surprise for me!"

music and barbecue evenings complete the casino's program of events. If, however, you have a private event to celebrate, you can also hire rooms at the building above the Limmat River for seminars, banquets, or weddings. Relax after one of the nerve-racking games with a stroll through the Casino's park, which is planted with mature trees.

E-Grand Tour of Switzerland

The E-Grand Tour is the world's first road trip for electric vehicles. A dense network of about 300 charging stations ensures power over the entire route and consequently guarantees comfortable and clean driving pleasure over its entire 1,000 mile (1,600km) length. Of course, you don't "have to" complete the entire tour to make use of the excellent charging infrastructure and to enjoy the landscape's beauty. Instead you can choose which of five alpine passes and which of the 22 lakes on the Grand Tour you would like to experience. And this is possible even if you do not own an EV—you can also hire a Tesla for the Tour.

Baden History Museum (approx. 1¼ miles/2km)

The Baden History Museum is located in the heart of the city, right by the Limmat River, and consists of the old Landvogtei (bailiwick) castle and a new building. While the reconstructed rooms of the bailiwick are dedicated to everyday life from the Middle Ages to the 20th century, the permanent "History connects" multi-media exhibition focuses on the city's spa and industrial history. As the exhibition's name implies, it uses numerous touch screens with text and visuals offering cross-references between the exhibits on show and explaining the contemporary historical context. In addition, two special exhibitions each year showcase socially relevant topics with a strong connection to the present day and to Baden itself.

Zurich by train (approx. 19 miles/30km)

The railroad station in Baden, which opened in 1847, is one of the oldest in Switzerland, and the station building itself is even the oldest in the country and still in operation. Here you can buy a ticket for the short journey to Zurich. Visit this beautiful city, the largest metropolis in federal Switzerland, and enjoy shopping at some of the most exquisite boutiques. If you want to enjoy a panoramic overview of the city, take the Uetlibergbahn (the S 10, part of the S-Bahn network) from Zurich train station up the local mountain, the Uetliberg. From here you can enjoy great views over the city, the Limmat River, and

↑ The high-caliber collection of Museum Langmatt in Baden appeals to more than just art connoisseurs. An intensive effort is being made to offer a program of workshops and entertaining museum tours for children. The children can borrow a museum's case full of search games as well as paper and color pencils for free—a unique chance to puzzle and paint.

↑ With 25 gaming tables for roulette, blackjack, and poker, plus well over 300 slot machines, there's no chance of boredom at the Grand Casino, which has been welcoming gamblers since 1891.

Lake Zurich. Especially in the summer, you might like the idea of going for a swim in these waters, and this is indeed possible anywhere in the city in one of the more than 40 Badis, as the bathing establishments are here called.

↑ Whether you dine or just come for a drink on the hotel's Eagle's Nest terrace, you'll always be able to enjoy the fabulous views of Vaduz Castle, seat of the Princes of Liechtenstein.

PARK HOTEL SONNENHOF
Vaduz, Liechtenstein

With its spectacular views and star-rated restaurant, the family-run Park Hotel Sonnenhof, above the capital city of Vaduz, provides a perfect retreat for business travelers and holidaymakers alike.

hotel info:

Park Hotel Sonnenhof
Mareestr. 29
FL-9490 Vaduz
Tel.: +423 2390202
Mail:
real@sonnenhof.li
Web:
www.sonnenhof.li

charging facilities:

1 Tesla DeC (Tesla only)
1 Tesla DeC (all EVs)

Just in time for the 300th anniversary of the Principality of Liechtenstein in 2019, Hubertus Real, the owner of the Park Hotel Sonnenhof, scored a coup on sustainability. To provide heating and air conditioning in the hotel, he installed two heat pumps, which derive their power largely from the hotel's own photovoltaic system. Started as Pension Sonnenhof by his parents in 1962, the Park Hotel is now environmentally future-proofed. Another aspect of the overall sustainability concept are the Tesla Destination Chargers. Of course, the hotel itself continues to impress with the quality of its 29 individual rooms as well as its spectacular hillside location above Liechtenstein's capital Vaduz. The hotel's superb wellness oasis with sauna and swimming pool is straight out of Arabian Nights. However, the ambience is instantly medieval in the extensive park and on the terrace, designed as an "Eagle's Nest," which grants you views of the princely castle. No wonder then, that this charming little boutique hotel is rated as one of the best family-run hotels in the world.

Mr T: *"Buy some of the Valle Dulcis sauces and chutneys. Made to the Marée recipes, they will recreate the holiday feeling at home."*

↑ The Sonnenhof's restaurant impresses with its tasteful decor and, even more so, with its outstanding cuisine.

Outstanding cuisine

The Marée Restaurant at the Sonnenhof also ranks among the very best of eateries, having been awarded one Michelin star and three Gault & Millau toques. Since 2019, a new design concept, relying entirely on lightness, elegance, and warmth, has been adopted, using precious natural materials such as bronze, leather, and walnut wood. Lightness and elegance also rule supreme in the Marée's cuisine. Here, top quality is assured by the owner himself. In 1988, Hubertus Real won a gold medal in the cookery category at the Sydney WorldSkills National Championships. Whether you're after one of the popular international classics, such as Asian-style marinated tuna, or a more regional special like glazed breast of pork from the Rhine Valley—the chef insists his valued guests are served only the best products, if possible from the immediate environment—seasonal, sustainable, and fresh.

AROUND VADUZ
Liechtenstein

A round trip through the sixth-smallest country in the world

The small Principality of Liechtenstein is nestled between Switzerland and the Rhine in the west and the Austrian Vorarlberg in the east, and is the mountainous home to 38,000 Liechtensteiners who are delighted to welcome visitors to their country.

Treasure Chamber Liechtenstein
(approx. ½ mile/1km)

One could almost say: "As befits a true principality ...," yet the Treasure Chamber of the Principality of Liechtenstein in Vaduz is housed in the Engländerbau, a former office building, and not in the castle.

On display are numerous exhibits from the Prince's collection, including gifts from kings and emperors, hunting equipment, and ancient weapons, and even several Fabergé eggs, which belonged to the estate of Adulf Peter Goop, a Liechtenstein patron of the arts. In organizational terms, the treasury is affiliated to the Liechtenstein National Museum. Its permanent exhibition is entitled "From the Principality to the World in Space," and so the collection also includes pieces of lunar rock from the Apollo 11 mission in 1969, which US President Richard Nixon gifted to the country.

Old Rhine Bridge
(approx. 1¼ miles/2km)

The Rhine, or the Alpine Rhine to be more precise geographically, forms the border between Liechtenstein and Switzerland. For over 70 years, the transportation of trade goods and passengers between the countries took place via ferry or wooden bridges, of which the Old Rhine Bridge between Vaduz and Sevelen in the canton of St. Gallen is the last remaining one. It was built in 1901 on the

Mrs T: "The perfect evening? Sitting with Mr T and a lovely glass of wine in the Eagle's Nest and taking in the sunset!"

five bridge pillars of a previous structure dating from 1870–71, and spans 443ft (135m). Until 1975, when a concrete bridge was built some 656ft (200m) down river, cars still drove across the Old Rhine Bridge, which has a closed roof and sides. Since then, the bridge has been reserved for non-motorized traffic and is popular with hikers and cyclists.

Museum of Art Liechtenstein
(approx. ½ mile/1km)

"Art in Cubes" is how the imposing buildings of the Liechtenstein art museums in Vaduz define themselves—a black cube, dating from 2000, and the directly adjacent Hilti Art Foundations white cube, built in 2015. In addition to their external shape, the two institutions are linked by the focus of their collections: modern and contemporary art. A museum of great structural simplicity, the starting point in 1967 was the gift of ten paintings; today; the museum focuses on sculptures, objets d'art, and (multimedia) installations. Solo exhibitions of internationally renowned artists like Joseph Beuys and Andy Warhol alternate with themed group exhibitions, with recent examples including, "Faites vos jeux! Art and Play since Dada" and "Time out. Art and Sustainability."

Gutenberg Castle
(approx. 5 miles/8km)

Gutenberg Castle is located in Liechtenstein's southernmost municipality of Balzers, about 15 minutes from Vaduz and the hotel. The complex, on a distinctively shaped hill, goes back to the High Middle Ages in the 13th century. In 1314, the castle fell to the Habsburgs, and in the Swabian War in 1499 it was unsuccessfully besieged by the Swiss Confederates. The castle fell into ruin in the aftermath, but was rebuilt in its present form in 1905–12. Its outer bailey is accessible all year round, and parts of the castle itself are used for cultural events and private occasions, such as wedding parties, from early May to late October. A guided tour of the castle can also be booked through the municipality, and the attractive garden and rose chapel open on Sundays.

Liechtenstein National Museum
(approx. ½ mile/1km)

As the name implies, everything at the Liechtenstein National Museum in the heart of Vaduz revolves around the history of the principality. The original collection comprises works of art and paintings, as well as medals and decorations, agricultural and alpine equipment, and historical weapons. A natural history collection in the museum's annex was added to the collections in

↑ All old: Gutenberg Castle was built over the course of the 13th century, and then heavily rebuilt in the early 16th century. The castle owes its resurgence after a period of decline to painter, sculptor, and architect Egon Rheinberger, who owned the castle from 1905 until his death in 1936.

↑ All new: The Kunstmuseum Liechtenstein is housed in two cubic structures—one black, the other white. Sculptures, objets d'art, and installations are exhibited in the buildings' grounds.

2003. In addition to the Postal Museum and the Treasury Chamber of the Principality of Liechtenstein, a traditional farmhouse museum in the Schellenberg community is also worth visiting.

GERMANY

BENEN-DIKEN-HOF

Keitum (Sylt), Germany

The Benen-Diken-Hof in Sylt's Keitum district is one of the last family-run hotels on Germany's most northerly island. The cluster of thatched houses that make up the complex feels like a picturesque "island on the island."

> Mr T: *"The hotel 'celebrates' electromobility—guests at the Benen-Diken-Hof will be picked up in the hotel's own Tesla."*

hotel info:

Benen-Diken-Hof
Keitumer Süderstr. 3-5
D-25980 Sylt-Keitum
Tel.: +49 4651 9383-0
Mail: info@benen-
diken-hof.de
Web: www.benen-
diken-hof.de

charging facilities:

2 Tesla DeC (Tesla only)
1 Tesla DeC (all EVs)
1 CEE 16 A
3-phase (all EVs)
1 CEE 32 A
3-phase (all EVs)

Some 985ft (300m) from the Wadden Sea, the sparsely populated district of Keitum on the island of Sylt is home to the lovely Benen-Diken-Hof, run by Claas-Erik Johannsen. Several thatched houses with a total of forty-eight rooms, suites, hotel-apartments, and studios surround the main building, which dates back to 1841. Lattice windows, oak or natural flooring create a traditional style, enhanced by the quality Friesian country-house furnishings. A particularly appealing touch is the fact that many rooms have their own terrace—the perfect place to relax in the fresh air. Claas-Erik Johannsen's friendly team manage to anticipate almost every guest requirement, and it is not long before the slogan on the wall, which roughly translates as "I am on Cloud 9," becomes a reality. You will also find yourself "floating" at the Wolkenlön Spa, with its large pool, sauna, and steam bath. After a relaxation session there, the regional fish and meat dishes at the Køkken restaurant will taste even better, as will the beer that is "spun" into the glass at the hotel bar, in keeping with an old family tradition.

AROUND KEITUM
Germany

Unspoilt nature and urbane living on Germany's most famous island

Sylt, one of the North Friesian islands, is well known for its shoreline's distinctive shape. But it is even better known for its beautiful countryside and long sandy beaches as well as chic shops and fancy hotels and some of the best restaurants in Germany. Sylt is the place to be!

List (approx. 12½ miles/20km)

List, on the island of Sylt, is Germany's most northerly municipality. It is a scenic hour's bike ride from the hotel, for which an e-bike is advisable, as a stiff westerly breeze tends to blow from the North Sea. Home to just under 1,500 people, the small town lies on the eastern side of the Wadden Sea, where a ferry operates to the nearby Danish island of Rømø. Vast shifting sand dunes extend across the inland area, while a sandy beach sweeps along the North Sea in the west (below). The red-and-white striped List-Ost lighthouse and the white List-West lighthouse act as perfect points of orientation—on land, sea, and from the air. And if you were arriving by air, you would immediately understand why the nearby peninsula containing Germany's northernmost point is referred to as the "Elbow."

Rantum Basin (approx. 2½ miles/4km)

The northern edge of the most biodiverse bird reserve in northern Germany is about a forty-five-minute walk from the hotel.

Named after the small town of Rantum, the *Rantumbecken*, or Rantum Basin, was cut off from the Wadden Sea by a dike constructed in 1937. The basin was originally intended as a landing site for hydroplanes. Today, some ten thousand birds gather among the 1,483 acres

Mrs T: "In the large spa area, everything is brandnew and inviting. Here you can easily sit back and just unwind!"

(600ha) area of reed beds, salt marshes, and swamps during the breeding or migration season. You are advised to have binoculars or a camera at the ready when hiking or cycling around here, for you will be able to spot dunlins, common terns, red knots, and many other species from the dike.

to eat

Since 1950, the artists' inn Kupferkanne, located in a pine grove in Kampen, has been a Sylt institution. You cannot really describe it, you have to experience it yourself! The décor alone looks like a mixture of paneled farmhouse parlor, beach bar, and airport lounge— and the rooms even incorporate a former bunker. The food served here includes a choice of hearty snacks from the sea or from the countryside as well as sweets in all variations, served with a home-roasted coffee or tea.

Kupferkanne
Stapelhooger Wai 7
D-25999 Kampen/Sylt
www.kupferkanne-kampen.de

↑ When the northern German evening chill sets in, the open fireplace in the Barefoot Hotel's lounge provides much-appreciated warmth and coziness.

BAREFOOT HOTEL

Timmendorfer Strand, Germany

People from all over the world in need of relaxation can recharge their own batteries at the Barefoot Hotel Timmendorfer Strand with its Long Island feel—while charging those of their electric cars at the same time!

hotel info:

Barefoot Hotel
Timmendorfer Strand
Schmilinsky Str. 2
D-23669 Timmendorfer
Strand
Tel.: +49 4503 76091000
Mail:
reservierungsanfrage
@barefoothotel.de
www.barefoothotel.de

charging facilities:

2 Tesla DeC (Tesla only)
1 Tesla DeC (all EVs)

The Barefoot Hotel Timmendorfer Strand stands a mere 656ft (200m) from the beach and the Baltic Sea. The hotel, with its wooden verandas and balconies, so closely resembles an American beach hotel, you can imagine yourself by the Atlantic, in the Hamptons on Long Island, perhaps, or by the Pacific near Malibu. In its design, actor, director, and producer Til Schweiger has combined the ambience of these two dream destinations. A bright building with soft colors, white wooden verandas and balconies, the hotel exudes a natural chic and soothing tranquility, well suited to its location right next to Timmendorf's peaceful spa park.

Mrs T: "The interior is perfectly in tune with its environment and, thanks to the natural colors and materials, triggers a warm sense of well-being."

A genuine feel-good atmosphere

The relaxed and informal atmosphere continues inside the Barefoot Hotel and its 57 rooms and suites. Wood from sustainable sources offers a beautiful backdrop on which to feature warm pastel colors and natural materials like pure wool and linen, while the rocking chairs on the verandas encourage you to forget about time pressures and lose yourself in the moment. You'll soon find yourself slipping off your everyday worries and cares together with your shoes and—as the hotel's name suggests—immersing yourself "barefoot" in your vacations. The hotel's culinary program also ensures its guests' perfect stay. Breakfast is served with a relatively late finishing time at 11:30 a.m., so no stress there. The first-class restaurant features regional specialties, and in the evening, a selection of excellent wines can be enjoyed on the terrace or in the lounge in front of the cozy fireplace.

The Barefoot's concept is rounded off by its excellent wellness and fitness facilities, including both a sauna and a spa area for pampering its guests. Yoga classes are always on the program, helping you unwind and recharge your internal batteries. The Barefoot Gym, meanwhile, features a range of cardio and other exercise equipment for your physical fitness. And, after a few relaxing days at the hotel, you may just feel that you really don't want to wear your shoes ever again.

↑ Comfortable wicker chairs and the light color of carpets, curtains, and covers create a friendly atmosphere.

↑ The spirit of the Hamptons on Long Island is not accidental—a stylish combination of American East Coast chic with the casual way of life on the Pacific side of the States is the concept at Til Schweiger's Barefoot Hotel.

Insight Barefoot Hotel

It was probably love at first sight, when German actor, Til Schweiger, saw a photograph of a building dating from the turn of the century 1900—an old beach house, exactly like the houses in Malibu or Long Island featuring wooden patios and verandas. After extensive renovations the building by the sea has been reinvented as a welcoming, chic hotel. Lots of wood, warm natural tones, and an organic touch of all surfaces— the holistic way of life is how Til Schweiger's concept can be summed up: authentic, full of character, and sustainable.

Uncomplicated, solid quality characterizes all other aspects of the hotel, including the wellness and fitness areas and the ↑ spacious balconies with their views to the dunes, the sea and the fine sandy beaches.

AROUND TIMMENDORFER STRAND
Germany

Chic baths, historic town centers, and a charming hinterland on the Baltic Sea

A visit to the Baltic Sea is a journey back in time to the late 19th century, with its Belle Époque grand hotels and even further back, to the prosperity of the Hanseatic cities. Return to the present at the Bird Park, on the High Ropes Trail, and at Sea Life.

to celebrate

Since the first concerts in 1986, the Schleswig-Holstein Music Festival has become one of the largest summer events for classical music in Europe. The basic idea was and still is to organize the performances in many different places, and also to select venues, such as country mansions, palace parks and even shipyards. The focus of the program is on an annually changing retrospective of a specific composer. This is supplemented by the performances of a musician, known as the "portrait artist" who will spend the entire festival summer in Schleswig-Holstein.
Schleswig-Holstein Music Festival
www.shmf.de
July–August

Sea Life Timmendorfer Strand (approx. 550yds/½km)

Between the Baltic Sea and the beach promenade lies the Sea Life Timmendorfer Strand, an aquarium covering an area of 16,146sq ft (1,500sq m). More than 2,500 animals live in different habitats, including a winter fjord, a harbor basin, a sea grass meadow, a rock grotto, and a tropical ocean, through which runs a glass underwater tunnel. Feeding takes place at different times of the day—for otters, rays, and sharks, even for the piranhas, which live in the waters of a small rainforest. Visitors can just drop into the small restaurant at the Sea Life for a delicious snack while enjoying the views of the Baltic Sea.

Lübeck (approx. 12½ miles/20km)

The "Queen of the Hanseatic League"—as Lübeck is also known—is about half an hour's drive to the south of the hotel. Situated on an island in the middle of the Trave River, the medieval old town is characterized by numerous buildings in the brick Gothic style, including the Holstentor with its two massive defensive towers, completed in 1478, and the St. Mary's Church built in the 13th and 14th centuries. Altogether, some 1,800 buildings are protected and the entire old town has been a UNESCO World Cultural Heritage site since 1987. For centuries, Lübeck was the capital of the Hanseatic League, a commer-

Mr T: "You can easily walk for a few hours along the beautifully developed beach promenade, preferably to Travemünde."

cial and defensive confederation of merchant guilds and market towns. So, it is not surprising that the plot of *Buddenbrooks*, Thomas Mann's 1901 society novel, revolves around the gradual decline of a merchant family in Lübeck. His grandparents' house in the old town now houses the Buddenbrookhaus, a literary museum well worth visiting.

High Ropes Tree Course Scharbeutz (approx. 1¼ miles/2km)

In the Kammerwald beyond the beaches of the Baltic Sea, less than half an hour's walk from the hotel, you'll find the forest high ropes course of Scharbeutz. From spring to fall, in good weather, you can master three different courses here between the trees. Their maximum heights are 8ft (2½m), 31ft (9½m), and 51ft (15½m), so everyone is catered for, from beginner to expert—even if you suffer from a fear of heights. Run over tree trunks, wobbly bridges, nets, seesaws, and rope runs; you'll have to balance, swing, and jump—always properly secured of course, and wearing sturdy shoes, gloves, and a safety belt.

Travemünde
(approx. 8 miles/13km)

Your car will take you from Timmendorfer Strand to Travemünde in about 20 minutes—but it's also a good destination for a long hike along the beach or, in some parts, on the steep, 33–66ft (10–20m) high Brodtener bank. Founded in 1187, Travemünde has been a district of Lübeck since 1913. Today, the town has two different faces: a medieval one including the Trave Promenade, the Old Bailiwick built in the style of the brick Renaissance, and the striking St. Lawrence Church; and a chic, maritime face centered around the lake promenade, the old lighthouse, and the white Maritim Hotel. The imposing four-masted barque "Passat" with its 184ft (56m) high masts lies at anchor in the Trave River, awaiting your visit. The route back for tired hikers is by bus.

Bird Park Niendorf Timmendorfer Strand
(approx. 3 miles/5km)

By car, it takes only 10 minutes to get to Bird Park Niendorf at Timmendorfer Strand, which is open all year round. The area, covering around 753,474sq ft (70,000sq m), lies in a reed landscape near the Aalbeek-Niederung nature reserve, and is considered the most important of its kind in Germany. The bird park is home to around 1,000 birds of 250 species, including flamingos and different types of owls, and also lesser-known birds like red-crowned cranes, goliath herons, the majestic Andes condor, and great hornbills. A

↑ In the evening light, Lübeck's civic pride is reflected in the Trave River. Characteristic stair gables grace the façades of the historic houses, several of which have been transformed into a museum.

↑ Summer vacation on the Baltic Sea, with your own wicker beach chair in the fine sand—it's the stuff the summer is made of. Accordingly, the beaches north of Lübeck are well frequented, especially in the area of the legendary Timmendorfer beach.

dense network of trails on both banks of the Dweerbeek River allows visitors access to the various aviaries, bird sanctuaries, and ponds as well as to the large free-flight aviary where herons, spoonbills, and glossy ibis can be seen.

↑ All the rooms (including the Paris room above) and apartments at the sevenoaks Hotel are warm and welcoming and individually decorated. It's so easy to feel at home here.

SEVENOAKS HOTEL
Cloppenburg, Germany

The sevenoaks Hotel in Cloppenburg in Lower Saxony impressively demonstrates that imagination, creativity, and style can turn any plain office building into a designer's dream.

hotel info:

sevenoaks Hotel
Museumstr. 8
D-49661 Cloppenburg
Tel.: +49 4471 8505845
Mail: info@
sevenoakshotel.de
Web: www.
sevenoakshotel.de

charging facilities:

2 Tesla DeC (Tesla only)
1 Tesla DeC (all EVs)

The motto of the small sevenoaks Hotel in Cloppenburg, which opened in March 2015, is: "A guest among friends—at home far-away." And this is the theme that runs through the entire complex, starting at reception. The latter consists simply of one desk—albeit a Thonet classic designed by Marcel Breuer. The breakfast area, with its large, 14-seat dining table, and the living room, with its cozy fireplace and well-stocked bookshelves, look and feel more like a private home than a classic hotel. They are distinguished by great attention to detail and an appealing mix of old and new.

Mrs T: *"The sevenoaks Hotel has managed to incorporate the whole world into its rooms in a creative way and with great style."*

↑ Sit on the sunny terrace and just relax with a good book or indulge in an extensive breakfast, which you can book in advance.

This is equally true of the eleven guest rooms, as each one has its own individual design. The only thing they all share is the high-quality natural bedding consisting of a variety of natural fibers obtained from renewable resources. Guests are spoiled for choice when it comes to bedroom design: would they prefer to spend their dusk-to-dawn hours in Mexico or Asia, in Paris or New York, the rainforest or France, the Hamptons or the Caribbean, the Orient, Africa, or the Alps? The world is your oyster. And to continue the hotel's concept of relaxed hospitality, the rooms have no minibar—you just help yourself to drinks, fruit, and even cake from the guest fridge or the espresso bar (and record your consumption on a notepad).

Would you prefer a stopover in Ibiza or Nantucket?

The sevenoaks room concept is complemented by seven one-bedroom apartments named Ibiza, Nantucket, Saltkorkan, Uppsala, Flandern, Rimini, and Little Britain. These "hideaways," each measuring about 646 sq ft (60 sq m), are also individually appointed and are fully equipped with a washing machine, dryer, and kitchenette, making them perfect for a one or two-week vacation with the whole family, or an extended business stay. For those traveling by EV, sevenoaks offers three Tesla Destination Chargers, which obtain some of their power from the building's solar units, photovoltaic systems and thermal ice storages—part of the hotel's all-encompassing sustainability concept.

AROUND CLOPPENBURG
Germany

Active relaxation
in the Oldenburger Münsterland

Surprisingly, neither Oldenburg nor Münster are located in the Oldenburger Münsterland, but they delineate the region to the north and to the south. Sandy heath and bog landscapes, forests and numerous lakes define this quiet, relaxing area.

Museum Village Cloppenburg (approx. 1¼ mile/2km)

The hotel may be located at Museumsstrasse, but the Cloppenburg Museum Village is about a twenty-minute walk away. One of the oldest of its kind, the museum village is dedicated to rural memories and everyday culture in the German state of Lower Saxony. It comprises some sixty historic buildings, including Low-Saxon hall and East Frisian Gulf houses. A school building and half-timbered church were also transported here in parts and reconstructed, as were a number of regional windmills. Also boasting a blacksmith's shop, a clog-making workshop, a saddlery, and other work premises, the museum village additionally provides information on once-common occupations, and visitors can watch artisans demonstrate their traditional crafts.

Quakenbrück (approx. 9 miles/15km)

The old town center of Quakenbrück, located several miles south, is dominated by over 100 historic half-timbered buildings from various centuries, known as *Burgmannshöfe*. First officially mentioned in 1235, Quakenbrück was initially a knights' stronghold that served to protect the Prince-Bishop's castle, before later becoming a member of the Hanseatic League. The main landmark, St. Sylvester's Church, with its striking round-topped spire, also dates back to the time of the town's found-

Mr T: "The sevenoaks hotel even generates the clean energy for charging our car itself—RESPECT!"

ing. St. Mary's Church, meanwhile, was erected in the second half of the 17th century on the foundations of a castle complex, its Neo-Gothic tower was not completed until 1873. Of Quakenbrück's five former city gates, only the Gothic Hohe Pforte from 1485 remains.

↑ When the beautifully presented dishes from Alexander Koppe's Michelin starred cuisine arrive on your Skykitchen table, you just won't know, whether to admire the views of Berlin or simply gaze at the artwork on your plate.

VIENNA HOUSE ANDEL'S BERLIN

Berlin, Germany

In the exciting East of Berlin the Vienna House Andel´s Berlin offers "bleisure"—that perfect mix of business and leisure. Holidaymakers, sightseers, and business travelers all feel equally at home here.

Hotelinfo:

Vienna House
Andel's Berlin
Landsberger Allee 106
D-10369 Berlin
Tel.: +49 30 4530530
Mail: info.andels-berlin
@viennahouse.com
Web:
www.viennahouse.com

charging facilities::

1 Tesla DeC (Tesla only)
3 Type 2 sockets (all EVs)
(own charging cable
required)

About 15 minutes away from Alexanderplatz, Berlin's pulsating heart, and just 164ft (50m) from the nearest S-Bahn station, the Vienna House Andel's Berlin is the ideal base from which to explore the city, as well as a welcoming haven of sustainability presented in a modern design. The 4-star superior hotel has 557 rooms and suites as well as large conference facilities, and places great emphasis on creating an environmentally friendly focus. The city center is easily accessible by public transport, bike, or e-scooter, while the underground parking lot has several charging stations for your e-vehicle. The hotel even boasts its own farmer's garden, with its organic products used in the restaurant, while its fresh kitchen herbs are grown in the hotel's small indoor garden. The rooms and suites themselves are styled in classic black-and-white, accentuated by pops of bright color.

Mr T: "Berlin is easy to explore from the hotel by public transport. If you prefer, you can also use an e-scooter or a bicycle instead."

Restaurants and bar—right up high

When it comes to dining, the hotel's three restaurants and bars make for a difficult choice. The Skykitchen serves French Michelin-star cuisine with an Asian twist and a shot of Berlin tradition—the chef himself comes from the German capital. You can also enjoy panoramic views of Berlin here, just as from Loft14, the hotel's stylish bar, where you have the choice of ordering a classic martini or one of the new Berlin mixology cocktails. The Mavericks restaurant, meanwhile, takes guests on a culinary and style journey, with an interior reminiscent of California's sunny surfing beaches—even on days when the sky above Berlin is not so blue.

The Vienna House Andel's Berlin also knows how to encourage its guests to combine wellness with energetic workouts; it boasts a 5,920 sq ft (550sq m) SpaSphere featuring a bio-sauna, Finnish sauna, steam bath, Jacuzzi, a number of different treatments (including anti-stress full-body massages), and of course state-of-the-art gym equipment—so no excuse there then. All this strenuous activity, and meanwhile your Tesla is idling away in the garage and "only allowed to recharge its battery."

↑ Of course, sustainability also means that there's a charging station for the guest' electric vehicles in the hotel's underground car park.

↑ There is so much to do in Berlin—but there's no need to rush around! You can see it all from your sun lounger as you relax on the terrace of the Vienna House Andel's Berlin enjoying a drink.

Insight Vienna House Andel's Berlin

It is rare for a business hotel to pay as much attention to sustainability as the Vienna House Andel's Berlin. Its technical facilities are powered by 100 percent renewable electricity, and since 2011 the hotel has several times been awarded the Green Globe Standard, which includes 44 core criteria supported by over 380 compliance indicators. A strict assessment is held every two years. There is also a friendly encouragement for guests to help—anyone who hangs an "environmental bag" on their door, indicating they don't need daily room cleaning therefore saving precious resources, will receive a "free green surprise," for example an organic apple.

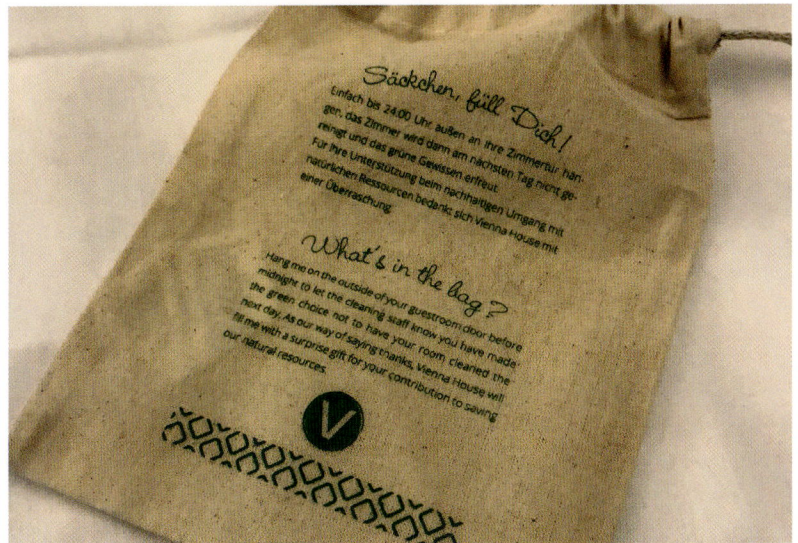

The hotel is careful not to pollute the environment. If you hang an environmental bag on the door, you waive the room cleaning ↑ for the day. Coziness and design are just as important.

AROUND BERLIN
Germany

German history up close

Since the rise of Prussia in the 18th and 19th centuries, German history has been concentrated around this vibrant capital. Its Museum Island is a major destination and the Berlin Wall's remains and Holocaust Memorial are testament to its turbulent past.

to celebrate

Founded in 1951, the Berlin International Film Festival, known as Berlinale for short, is the largest public festival in the world with over 300,000 tickets sold. The Berlinale Palast on Potsdamer Platz and other cinemas in the city center project some 400 movies, of which 20 enter the competition for the coveted Golden and Silver Bears. Numerous other movie series, such as the International Forum of New Cinema, a retrospective of Berlinale Classics, and a series for short films round off the silver screen spectacular.
Belinale
www.berlinale.de
February

Museum Island (approx. 2½ miles/4km)

Museum Island, in the heart of the Berlin-Mitte district, boasts five major museums founded between 1830 and 1930, and is today a UNESCO World Heritage Site. Heading north past the Cathedral, you will first come to the the Altes Museum (Old Museum), with its Antiquities collection. Beyond the colonnade, you will see the Neues Museum (New Museum) on your left, which features Egyptian exhibits such as the stirring bust of Nefertiti, and on your right the Alte Nationalgalerie (Old National Gallery), with a predominantly 19th-century collection. Marking the end of the precinct are the U-shaped Pergamon Museum, with original ancient structures from the Middle East, and finally the Bode Museum, with its striking dome, which holds a sculpture collection and Byzantine exhibits.

Hackesche Höfe (approx. 2 miles/3km)

Not far from Alexanderplatz is one of Berlin's finest early 20th-century architectural complexes: the Hackesche Höfe. Built in 1906, it encompasses eight courtyards surrounded by some 6¾ acres (27,000sq m) of commercial and residential premises. With exteriors reflecting the Eclecticism of the Wilhelmine era, some of the courtyards feature surprisingly fanciful Art Nouveau elements. Heritage-listed in 1977, while still part of East Germany, the Hackesche Höfe were exten-

Mrs T: "There can surely be no more perfect view of the skies over the great city of Berlin than that from the Skykitchen!"

sively restored in the mid-1990s. Today, they house a number of small businesses, restaurants, the Hackesche-Höfe-Kino Cinema, and the Chamäleon Theater.

Berlin Wall Memorial (approx. 3 miles/5km)

The Berlin Wall Memorial, located in the middle of the city, is a reminder of the divided city from the Construction of the Wall on August 13, 1961 to its Fall on November 9, 1989. A 230ft (70m) long section of the original concrete wall has been rebuilt, along with border strips and an original watchtower, which can be viewed from the platform of the documentation center directly opposite.

Berlin Currywurst
(approx. 2½ miles/4km)

Can a sausage be considered a tourist attraction? In any case, this particular sausage with curry ketchup is sold at numerous stands all over Berlin—you simply cannot escape it. If you want to try one in style, head to Konnopke's Imbiss under the U-Bahn track on Schönhauser Allee. It's somewhat of a cult site as this was the first place in Germany to sell currywurst in 1930.

Charlottenburg Palace
(approx. 7½ miles/12km)

Charlottenburg Palace, and its baroque palace garden, is a magnificent complex situated in the west of Berlin. First built in 1699 as a small palace for Sophie Charlotte of Hannover, the wife of Frederick III, the last elector of Brandenburg, who, as Frederick I, became the first king of Prussia. Following his early death in 1705, the palace was christened Charlottenburg, and underwent extensions by various rulers until 1797. In the final construction phase in 1824–25, a pavilion was built near the main façade. The palace is just a short car ride from the lush Havelland district, which you can explore en route to the famous citadel of Spandau.

Berlin Jewish Museum
(approx. 3¾ miles/6km)

The Berlin Jewish Museum, located in the district of Kreuzburg, is Europe's largest Jewish museum, covering more than 1,700 years of German-Jewish history. Its permanent exhibition is housed in a zigzag extension building designed by Daniel Libeskind, which is connected to the museum's baroque entrance via an underground walkway. The Garden of Exile has forty-nine concrete stelae planted with olive trees—forty-eight in Berlin soil and one in soil from Jerusalem. The unsettling Holocaust Tower is

↑ Serious: Daniel Libeskind's extension of the Jewish Museum has been much discussed and mostly admired. The architecture succeeds in satisfying practical and aesthetic requirements while at the same time preserving the character of a memorial site.

↑ Playful: In the Charlottenburg Palace park, visitors today are greeted by putti, just like Sophie Charlotte for whom it was built, and later Frederick the Great, who made the palace his main residence for a few years, before moving to quieter village of Potsdam.

almost totally dark inside, a reminder of the genocide committed by the Nazis. The neighboring W. Michael Blumenthal Academy houses the museum's library and archive.

↑ Molecule Man dances on the Spree River, with the Berlin skyline in the background.

↑ Guests can enjoy exquisite cuisine at the Schwarzer Adler gourmet restaurant, where head chef Christian Baur works in perfect harmony with his predecessor, Anibal Strubinger.

FRANZ KELLER SCHWARZER ADLER

Vogtsburg-Oberbergen (Kaiserstuhl), Germany

The Hotel Schwarzer Adler in Oberbergen is a culinary stronghold, and together, the hotel, restaurant, and associated vineyard offer guests an exclusive and welcoming center for relaxation and well-being in Südbaden.

hotel info:

Hotel Schwarzer Adler
Badbergstr. 23
D-79235 Vogtsburg-
Oberbergen
Tel.: +49 7662 9330-0
Mail:
keller@franz-keller.de
Web:
www.franz-keller.de

charging facilities:

2 Tesla DeC (Tesla only)
1 Tesla DeC (all EVs)

In Vogtsburg-Oberbergen, the members of the Fritz Keller family have all personally cared for their guests' well-being for more than 100 years. The kitchen at the Schwarzer Adler gourmet restaurant has had a Michelin star since 1969, when Irma Keller was the first female chef in Germany to receive that honor. The restaurant is rich in traditions, heavily influenced by French cuisine, being located so close to the border. The multi-course top menu is matched by the excellent white and red wines from the in-house winery, headed by the Kellers' son, Friedrich. The wine list featuring 2,700 wines is outstanding. Part of the parent company is the Hotel Schwarzer Adler, where hospitality is writ large, as in the nearby Rebstock vintner's inn "Im Weinberg." The standard, deluxe, and superior double rooms are all furnished in a modern and elegantly tasteful design. Equally ultra-modern is the hotel's destination charger—after all, the host himself is a Tesla driver.

Mr T: "You should book a room here—not just because of the hotel's top-quality wines, but also because of its rich and varied cuisine."

Vintners, hosts, wine merchants

The Keller family is totally committed to the triple motto of "vintners, hosts, wine merchants," yet you won't necessarily have to get into your Tesla to reach the other destinations in the group—a short walk through the village is sufficient. High-quality down-to-earth fare is served at the Rebstock across the road, a basic but cozy vintners' eatery. Local dishes from the Baden and Alsace regions and seasonal specialities, such as dandelion leaf salad, are served here to appreciative locals, hikers, and day-trippers alike. A more stylish venue is the KellerWirtschaft. Less than 2,000ft (600m) away, this vineyard restaurant opened in 2013 is designed to reflect the contours of the Kaiserstuhl vineyard terraces. Wine and food are perfectly matched in this beautiful restaurant where you can relax by the flickering flames in the open fireplace and take in the stunning views of the Kaiserstuhl vineyards through panoramic windows. Make sure before you leave the hotel you stock up on your favorite wine at the vinotheque.

↑ A visit of the vineyard is a must. Your freshly charged Tesla can then transport a few "liquid souvenirs" back home.

Insight Franz Keller Schwarzer Adler

Fritz and Friedrich Keller make all the important decisions together at the Franz Keller winery. Their concern is the cultivation of full-bodied Burgundy wines and the growing conditions that are the basis for a perfect wine including the care and maintenance of the steep, terraced slopes. Their wine-making approach has been inspired by the wines of neighboring France and they are driven by an uncompromising, consistent quality awareness that begins in the vineyard. An environmentally friendly, gentle viticulture and a reduction of the yield produce top wines that are fresh and fruity yet complex, mineral-rich, and full-bodied.

↑ The panoramic windows of the KellerWirtschaf reveal the view of the historic vineyards on the slopes of the Oberbergener Bassgeige to diners. In the summer, the hosts grill on the terrace once a week.

AROUND VOGTSBURG
Germany

Where Germany and France meet. A food-lover's paradise!

Germany's extreme southwest not only enjoys a favorable climate, it's also a center of culinary excellence. You would be hard-pushed to find as many stars, toques, or simply outstanding restaurants anywhere else. The culinary impact of nearby France, which is just the other side of the Rhine, is a major influence.

Freiburg im Breisgau
(approx. 12½ miles/20km)

Going south, we arrive at the southernmost city in Germany, Freiburg im Breisgau. On a tour of the old town, which is criss-crossed by "Bächle," or water gullies, and has numerous cafés and shops, you'll find the Albert Ludwig University, founded in the medieval city in 1457. After World War II, the center was rebuilt to its historical dimensions. The old town is dominated by the Gothic Minster and its 380ft (116m) high spire. On Münsterplatz stands the ox-blood-red Historisches Kaufhaus, or Historical Merchants' Hall, with life-size figures of Habsburg emperors, and a picturesque market takes place around the Minster during the week. Towering over the town and the Minster is the Schauinsland, the 4,213ft (1,284m) high "local" mountain, which is accessible by cable car.

Vitra Design Museum
(approx. 43 miles/70km)

Located in Weil am Rhein is the Vitra Design Museum of the eponymous manufacturer of contemporary designer furniture. Opened in late 1989, the building was designed by Canadian-American architect and designer Frank O. Gehry, the first of his buildings in Europe. Since then, parts of the extensive collection of furniture and interiors has been

Mrs T: "In winter the KellerWirtschaft hosts concerts, and in summer they delight their guests with barbecues on the terrace."

shown in temporary exhibitions on the life and work of industrial or furniture designers and architects, a veritable *Who's who* of the industry: retrospectives here have focused on Charles and Ray Eames, Verner Panton, Marcel Breuer, Ludwig Mies van der Rohe, Frank Lloyd Wright, and also on Frank O. Gehry.

↑ As soon as guests enter the lobby and reception area of the Öschberghof, they immediately relax in this open, bright, and modern hotel.

ÖSCHBERGHOF

Donaueschingen, Germany

Situated on the edge of the Black Forest, the Öschberghof, newly revamped as a luxury resort, combines world-class golf courses, state-of-the-art spas, and upscale gastronomy: everything to make the heart beat faster!

hotel info:

Öschberghof
Golfplatz 1
D-78166
Donaueschingen
Tel.: +49 771 84-0
Mail: info@
oeschberghof.com
Web: www.
oeschberghof.com

charging facilities:

5 DeC (all EVs)

Positioned in the gentle hills on the outskirts of Donaueschingen stands the Öschberghof, a spacious five-star superior resort, easily accessible by Tesla via the A 81, and a good starting point for excursions to the nearby Black Forest. The Öschberghof offers its guests exquisite, modern, and stylish rooms and suites, featuring large picture windows with views of the lush green golf course. Your culinary needs are also well catered for. There are a total of four restaurants and bars at the Öschberghof, and among these, the ÖSCH NOIR in the main building raises gastronomy to a new level. Manuel Ulrich's cuisine features excellent French dishes with a modern take, and head sommelier Michael Häni will recommend one of the cellar's 700 exclusive wines for a perfect match. In the Öventhütte, things are a little more rustic. Located a short way away under Black Forest firs and furnished in the style of a typical mountain lodge, the menu at this restaurant features hearty local meals as well as tasty specialties from the open-air barbecue.

A wellness paradise

If you're looking for relaxation, the 53,820sq ft (5,000sq m) ÖSCH SPA is the right place. It's divided into four experience zones, named Harmony, Energy, Asia, and Lady SPA—the latter being a withdrawal zone exclusively reserved for female guests. In the Harmony Spa, a salt rock wall and the Microsalt system provide soothing revitalization and freshness. The salty air cleans the airways and can help with allergic reactions. The Energy Spa comprises the hotel's saunas: the 388sq ft (36sq m) event sauna and the 360-degree sauna with fully glazed panoramic views. In addition, there is an infrared cabin and a steam bath, as well as experience showers and an ice lounge, which offers the perfect way to cool down after a sauna. The Asia Spa also features a sauna, a steam bath, and an *onsen*. A Far Eastern interior design, decorative lanterns, and bamboo pillars, create a discreet, therapeutic, and all-round calming ambience.

> *Mr T:* "Well, I'm bowled over! Even if the Öventhütte with its large outdoor grill is not in the Bavarian mountains."

↑ Enjoy the rare hours of winter sunshine by the infinity outdoor pool with brine, and then have a relaxing swim—the water is heated throughout the year.

↑ The 18-hole East Course, which was opened in May 2017, comprises six ponds. In addition, a stream and a water meadow landscape have been integrated into the design of the course. From Hole 10 you can enjoy spectacular views of the Feldberg.

Insight Öschberghof

The architecture of the hotel's fine dining restaurant, the ÖSCH NOIR, reflects a modern interpretation of the Black Forest traditions with a clever use of light and shade creating a relaxed environment. The kitchen run by Chef Manuel Ulrich relies on excellent French food with modern influences. Head sommelier Michael Häni recommends the wine, which will perfectly round off and complement each dish on the outstanding menu. With Häni's expert guidance, you can choose the perfect bottle from more than 700 national and international wines and begin an exciting new journey into the fascinating world of wines.

The hotel's spa complex covers an area of 53,820sq ft (5,000sq m), but you can also simply relax in its spacious rooms and ↑ suites. Your stay will be rounded off, if you like, with the upscale gastronomy at the ÖSCH NOIR.

AROUND DONAUESCHINGEN
Germany

Where Breg and Brigach join to make the Danube

Between Swabian Alb and Black Forest lies the town of Donaueschingen, at the confluence of the Danube's two sources. Excursions to the surrounding low mountain ranges can be combined with visits to the town's main attractions.

Fürstlich Fürstenbergischer Park
(approx. 2½ miles/4km)

Located in the city center of Donaueschingen is the Princely Fürstenberg Park, also known as Donaueschingen Palace Park. The sprawling complex was created around 1820 in the then popular style of French and English landscape gardens in the marshes near the Brigach River. Under the motto "Once the home of frogs, now of health," the park adjoining the baroque Fürstenberg Palace is open to the public. Featuring Germany's oldest Lessing monument and a fish house in the style of a Greek temple, the Danube spring, housed in a round enclosure, is a good starting or end point for a walk through the grounds. The source of the Danube Stream, which flows into the Brigach River after only 328ft (100m), is, together with the Brigach and the other source, the Breg River, one of the origins of the Danube.

Museum Art.Plus
(approx. 2½ miles/4km)

Donaueschingen's Museum Art.Plus is also located close to the palace on the Brigach River. Based in a Classicist building dating from 1841, it shows a small but expertly curated number of contemporary art works, including large sculptures in the garden along the riverbank. In addition to the annually changing group exhibition, the Museum Art. Plus also aims to show three solo exhibitions

Mrs T: "The Öeschberghof has been one of my absolute top-favorite wellness hotels for very many years now."

a year. Showcasing works by artists of international renown, as well as the creative output of local artists, visitors will always be sure find new and inspiring exhibits.

Villingen
(approx. 11 miles/18km)

The Baden side of the twin town of Villingen-Schwenningen, created in 1972 during municipal reforms, boasts a well-preserved medieval old town. Divided into four districts by a large crossroads—a layout typical of a Zähringer town—it is encircled by an almost complete city wall with three stately gates: the Oberes Tor, the Riettor, and the Bickentor. The old town also has the early-Gothic

The town of Rottweil is located 20 miles (32km) from the hotel, in the direction of Stuttgart. The annual highlight during the Swabian-Alemannic carnival, locally known as Fasnet, is the so-called Narrensprung, or Fool's Jump. When the clocks chime 8 a.m. on Shrove Monday, the fools start jumping though a gate in the old town', the Schwarzes Tor. In addition to the friendly Gschell with his smooth larva (mask), there are also the grim-looking Biss, the Schantle with his plucking suit, and the Federahannes in his feathered coat, who jumps over his big stick. The Narrensprung is repeated on Shrove Tuesday at 8 a.m. and 2 p.m. And at all three occasions, spectators need to be on guard so that they will not be reprimanded by the fools for any of the previous year's municipal incidents.

Rottweiler Narrensprung
www.rottweil.de
Shrove Monday

↑ What rises as the source of the Danube inside a round framework featuring sculptural decorations in the Donaueschingen Palace Park is rainwater, "bursting" from the karstic rock. The resulting Donaubach flows almost immediately into the Brigach, which after another 4,593 ft (1,400m) joins up with the Brig to create the Danube.

Minster of Our Lady, built in the 13th to 15th century, and remodeled in the baroque style in the 18th century, as well as the late-Gothic city hall dating from 1534. Also worth seeing are the Franziskaner Museum, presenting city and regional history, and the Zehndersches Haus, a timber-framed building from 1690.

Öschberghof Golf Course

You don't have to be a triathlete, but a certain degree of fitness would definitely not go amiss on the unique 45-hole Öschberghof Golf Course! The holes may be a challenge but at least the tees were designed to save your efforts, as they are all a maximum of five minutes from the resort. The challenging 18-hole Old Course has been in existence since 1975. It is located in a parkland planted with a variety of trees. The East Course, inaugurated in 2017, also has 18 holes; the tenth hole is the most beautiful one because it grants you panoramic views of the Feldberg Mountain in the Black Forest. Finally, the 9-hole Academy Course is the place for a quick lap in between. Sustainability is a high priority for the course operator and the course is certified by the self-regulatory and pro-active environmental

"Golf & Nature" management system, developed by the German Golf Association (DGV).

Triberg Waterfalls
(approx. 25 miles/40km)

The Triberg Waterfalls, considered to be Germany's highest and best-known waterfalls, are found right in the heart of the Black Forest. They have been a popular tourist destination since tourists began visiting the region over 150 years ago. This is where the Gutach River, having emerged from several springs on the Schönwald Plateau, plunges into the depths over two cascade sections and a total drop of 535ft (163m). Well-developed hiking trails and two wooden bridges give access to the waterfalls, at the same time offering ever-new perspectives on them. The waterfalls are particularly spectacular to see in the spring, as they carry a torrent of water when the snows melt, as well as every evening, as they are floodlit until 10 p.m.

HOTEL MÜNCHEN PALACE
Munich, Germany

The München Palace offers all the amenities you would expect from a large luxury hotel, but it does so in an impressively exquisite boutique style. It is no wonder that it counts many regulars among its guests.

hotel info:

München Palace
Trogerstr. 21
D-81675 Munich
Tel.: +49 89 41971-0
Mail: info@hotel-muenchen-palace.de
Web: www.hotel-muenchen-palace.de

charging facilities:

2 Tesla DeC (Tesla only)
1 Tesla DeC (all EVs)

The München Palace is a luxury boutique hotel in Munich's Bogenhausen district near the Prinzregenten Theater. Behind its rather unobtrusive exterior lies an almost unparalleled level of exclusivity—an oasis in the heart of the city. The eighty-nine rooms, including fifteen suites, are traditionally and tastefully appointed with great attention to detail, and all materials are of exquisite quality. Particularly striking is the view of the quiet, romantic interior courtyard, where, on clear days, you can sit and enjoy the delicious breakfast of local and seasonal produce. Evenings are best spent in the Palace Bar, which ranks as one of Munich's best

Mrs T: "The style of the hotel fits its Munich environs, and if you like traditions, dirndls, and lederhosen, then you're definitely in the right place anyway."

hotel bars, and which is also popular among night owls heading back from places such as the Prinzregenten Theater. Alternatively, try the Palace Restaurant, which serves specialties unique to the owners (the Kuffler family), such as beef from the Lake Tegernsee region. Throughout the Palace, you will notice how attentively the hotel team caters to its guests' needs. Even if it is your first time here, you will be looked after as if it were your hundredth.

AROUND MUNICH
Germany

Economic engine with a feel-good factor

Even in winter, the countless street cafés in the Bavarian capital fill up in no time as soon as the sun shines. Germany's third city is an intriguing mix of museums, Neo-Gothic architecture, the annual Oktoberfest, elegant city stores and, of course, the famous glockenspiel show.

Viktualienmarkt (approx. 2 miles/3 km)

The Viktualienmarkt is located on the southeastern edge of Munich's historic center. Food has been sold here at numerous stalls since 1807, so there is nothing stopping you from savoring a hearty Bavarian Brotzeit snack—try a white veal sausage with sweet wholegrain mustard, pretzels, and black radish. Or simply head to one of the beer gardens and order a cool beer to drink with your *Brotzeit*—enjoy it under the watchful eye of life-like statues of local greats such as humorists Karl Valentin, Liesl Karlstadt, and Weiss Ferdl. The Dance of the Market Women is held every Shrove Tuesday as part of the city's carnival season. The women are joined by spectators who also dress up in traditional costumes in this colorful and exuberant celebration.

The English Garden (approx. ½ mile/1km)

The English Garden is one of the largest urban parks in the world, and it was also one of the first to be accessible and enjoyed by the entire population as early as 1789. Extensive lawns, on which famously the *Nackerten* (nudists) romp in summer, alternate with a wide variety of different tree species, and the park is crossed by water courses and lakes. The locals and their guests stroll through the extensive grounds on its countless paths, visit the small

Mr T: "Munich is always worth a visit and the annual visit of the Wiesn during the Oktoberfest is a personal highlight!"

Monopteros, which offers beautiful vistas of the city, take a Brotzeit, a hearty local snack in the beer garden, enjoy drinks and delicious meals at one of the restaurants, or wander to the famous Eisbachwelle, where the experienced, the courageous, and the crazy brave the rushing waters on their surfboards.

to celebrate

The Oktoberfest is the world's largest popular festival. In addition to the stalls and entertainments, it is above all the huge beer tents where plenty of beer is consumed and live music played that attract up to seven million visitors from around the world to Munich each year.

Oktoberfest end September

to eat

One of the most rustic and typically Bavarian inns is the Nürnberger Bratwurst-Glöckl near the Frauenkirche in the city center. It lives up to its name with the house specialty: sausages in many variations, grilled over a beech wood fire.

Nürnberger Bratwurst Glöckl am Dom Frauenplatz 9 D-80331 Munich www.bratwurst-gloeckl.de

SCANDINAVIA

MEJERI GAARDEN

Gedser, Denmark

If you are looking for a carefully managed small hotel in a beautiful location in the south of Denmark, you will find it at Mejeri Gaarden, one of those rare places where holidaymakers, travelers, and locals feel at ease.

Mejeri Gaarden is a charming bed and breakfast guesthouse on Falster Island, south of Copenhagen. The hotel was once a thriving dairy farm and its country location, surrounded by fields, woods and parkland is secluded and quiet. The estate has since been meticulously revamped by owners Michael and John. The focus here is on "quality, not quantity," and this is immediately made apparent by the fact that its six guest rooms are all individually and tastefully decorated, with each room featuring a different color scheme that is reflected in the room name. There is additional accommodation in a comfortable, newly renovated cottage, situated a short distance away. The authenticity theme is continued in the restaurant, where traditional, locally sourced dishes are served. The menu is short but of a high standard. And for some cultural variety, the beautifully restored conference venue hosts special events. Taking a relaxed stroll on the private road to the sheltered beach is an absolute must; from here you'll be able to experience some spectacular sunsets.

> Mrs T: "Every detail was taken care of in the hotel. Artworks adorn the walls and a spiral staircase takes you to the rooms on the upper floor."

AROUND GEDSER
Denmark

The most southerly corner

The two islands of Falster and Lolland, separated by the narrow Guldborgsund, form the southernmost part of Denmark. The wide, flat landscape—the highest point of Falster is just 144ft (44m) above the sea—is the ideal basis for winding down and rest and rejuvenation.

Gedser Odde (approx. 6¾ miles/11km)

Mejeri Gaarden is located in the district of Gedser, where ferries moor after making the 28 mile (45km) journey from Rostock in Germany. Another 2 miles (3km) farther south of Gedser is Gedser Odde, the southernmost point of Denmark (below), as well as of Scandinavia itself. A short wooden staircase leads down the 20–26ft (6–8m) high cliff to the sea, where you can soak up the tranquility and lapping waves, watch the sun set over the water in the west, and, depending on the season, observe the migratory birds. A quick run or jog along the seemingly endless beach at the eastern end of Falster to the charming town of Marielyst is another exceptionally enjoyable experience.

Knuthenborg Safaripark (approx. 29 miles/47km)

Established in 1969, the Knuthenborg Safaripark is the largest safari and theme park in Northern Europe. It has more than 9 miles (15km) of drivable roads and is home to more than 900 animals. There are many designated spots where you can get out of the car and experience the wilderness up close. The park's fauna is organized by continent; the Savanna section is dominated by African species such as zebras, giraffes, ostriches, antelopes, gnus, and rhinos, and the Asian animals include water buffalo, yaks, and, in particular, the

Mr T: "The journey to Mejeri Gaarden is a delight, and three destination chargers are available in the beautiful courtyard."

rare Siberian tiger, which is kept in its own enclosure. Kangaroos and emus represent the native animals of Australia, and bison and moose the prairies of North America. A nature playground rounds off the adventure for younger visitors, while the café and restaurant is open to everyone.

SKT. PETRI
Copenhagen, Denmark

Design meets sustainability. The Skt. Petri Hotel offers environmentally friendly luxury in the center of Denmark's busy capital city as well as an excellent starting point for sightseeing.

hotel info:

Hotel Skt. Petri
Krystalgade 22
DK-1172 København
Tel.: +45 33 459100
Mail: stay@
sktpetri.com
Web: www.
sktpetri.com

charging facilities:

1 Tesla DeC (Tesla only)
1 Tesla DeC (all EVs)

Skt. Petri Hotel is situated in the picture-postcard historic center of Copenhagen, which is considered one of the world's most eco-friendly cities. Its Modernist exterior opens up to the laid-back luxury of the stylish, grandly-proportioned lobby which is dominated by the color green—an indication of the hotel's commitment to sustainability, which is shared by the city itself. The hotel's power is wind-generated, food waste is collected for conversion to biofuel, palm oil is banned, the chef only uses certified fish, and guests are given the option of refusing housekeeping services, for which the hotel in return donates 50 kroner a day to

Mr T: "It is ecologically sensible to explore this bustling city directly from the hotel on foot or by bike—the bikes can also be hired at the hotel."

UNICEF. Scandinavian style plus great attention to detail have created stunning rooms in shades of blue and gold. Modern design, along with delicious food and drink, is the hallmark of the Petri Restaurant & Bar and the Dada Restaurant. Open from midday onward, Petri serves international cuisine and "mini bites," while at Dada, which opens for dinner, the menu is inspired by Middle Eastern and Mediterranean cooking.

AROUND COPENHAGEN
Denmark

Stress-free exploration of Denmark's capital

Scandinavian cities have a personality of their own. Although the city is very lively, and many Danes share this small area, it never feels crowded, stressful, or noisy. Everything ticks along in a calm, relaxed fashion—an excellent combination that both stimulates and relaxes local people and visitors.

Nyhavn (approx. ½ mile/1km)

Heading south, Nyhavn is just a short stroll from the hotel, across the central square known as Kongens Nytorz, though the "new harbor," completed in 1673, is actually an old branch canal. The colorful 17th and early 18th century gabled buildings serve as a back-drop for historic wooden ships moored in the water, while the 17th and early 18th century buildings house cafés, bars, and restaurants, making the district around Nyhavn one of Copenhagen's liveliest dining and entertainment areas. The stunning waterfront has often been used as a film set! As you stroll east down the car-free, 1,312ft (400m) long Nyhavn, you will see to your left beyond the port basin a building with an exquisite fusion of architectural styles: the futuristic new opera house.

Tivoli (approx. ½ mile/1km)

The Tivoli, on the edge of downtown Copenhagen, opened in 1843, making it the second oldest amusement park in the world. Its particular charm lies in the fact that new attractions are introduced every year and

sit comfortably alongside the old-fashioned popular wooden *Rutschebanen* rollercoaster dating from 1914, and the Chinese-style *Pantomimeteatret*, an open-air stage that was first used in 1874. Over twenty different rides—including a 262ft (80m) high swing

Mrs T: "The hotel provides tips on how to save resources—for example, by drinking the clean Copenhagen tap water."

carousel— and more than thirty restaurants promise an entertaining day at the Tivoli and the lush greenery of the gardens offers a peaceful contrast to the busy rides. The park is open every day from mid-April to the end of September, over the festive period and on special public holidays.

to eat

The Standard is a restaurant concept that combines four restaurants under the roof of an elongated, former Art Deco customs house and ferry terminal on Havnegade quay: the Almanak with modern Nordic cuisine, the Mission with vegetarian Mediterranean-Californian dishes, the Studio with Michelin-starred gourmet cuisine, and The Standard's Private Dining for exclusive events such as business meetings or weddings.

The Standard
Havnegade 44
DK-1058 Copenhagen
www.thestandardcph.dk

↑ The Nivå 84 sits on a rock formation 276ft (84m) above the lake, and resembles a very beautifully-designed lookout point. An architectural experiment that its guests are delighted to be part of!

NIVÅ 84 LOFT HOUSE
Trånghalla, Sweden

The small but perfect Nivå 84 Loft House boutique hotel is a stylish retreat for couples looking to enjoy spectacular views of Sweden's second largest lake, Lake Vättern.

hotel info:

Nivå 84 Loft House
Skogsbostigen 5
S-564 36 Trånghalla
(Bankeryd)
Tel.: +46 730 894412
Mail: via airbnb contact facility
Web: www.airbnb.de/rooms/13583879

charging facilities:

1 Tesla DeC (Tesla only)
1 CEE 16A
3-phase (all EVs)

Good things come in small packages, as the saying goes, though in the case of Nivå 84 Loft House, it would be even more apt to say that "the best of things come in the tiniest of packages." Nivå 84, which is managed by Carl-Johan Lundberg and his wife Eleonor, is not a hotel as such, but rather a loft house—comprising precisely one room! But what a room it is! Built next to the hosts' own home, the modern Nivå 84 cube sits on a cliff exactly 276ft (84m) above Lake Vättern. Facing east over the lake, giant panoramic windows open up the building, providing a spectacular view of the sunrise over the water from both the living and sleeping areas. And after an eventful day exploring the surroundings, you can enjoy watching the sun set from the west-facing modern terrace lounge.

Mr T: *"Tesla features extra-large in this place—because, in terms of statistics, there is one Destination Charger for each room!"*

Design loft for couples

Once inside the dramatic Nivå 84 Loft House, you will feel as if you are in a photo shoot for a design magazine. When it comes to the interior décor, the Lundbergs have specifically focused on striking a stylish yet harmonious contrast between the pale wood of the building and the black furnishings. Even the tiles in the bathroom, which features a rain shower, have a wood-like texture to continue the theme. A small work area is equipped with high-speed Internet and USB chargers in the living area downstairs, and the mezzanine sleeping area with its double bed, accessed via a staircase, boasts a sound system and a flat-screen television with a streaming connection for guests' audiovisual entertainment. There is also a sofabed so you can accommodate up to two more people. Guests can prepare a delicious meal on the gas barbecue on the balcony from where you overlook the lake or—for breakfast or small snacks—use Nivå 84's coffee machine, toaster, egg cooker, and microwave in the kitchenette. If you need anything else, the perfect hosts next-door will do their best to help out. By the time you are back in your Tesla, you will be revitalized and full of energy, although a little sad to leave the warm hospitality behind.

↑ You can watch the fascinating spectacle of the Scandinavian twilight for hours directly from the window in your room.

↑ The "balcony" is actually a terrace, but it goes steeply downhill directly behind it. Thanks to the glass closure you don't have to be free of vertigo to enjoy breakfast and dinner with a view over the lake.

AROUND TRÅNGHALLA
Sweden

In Astrid Lindgren's picture-book Sweden

Lake Vättern, the second largest lake in Sweden is the jewel at the center of this beautiful region with its lush green meadows, dense forests, and picturesque old towns. The area also benefits from a perfect infrastructure, which makes driving around the countryside in an e-mobile pure joy.

Jönköping
(approx. 4 miles/6km)

Jönköping (below right), located at the southern end of Lake Vättern, is the nearest town to the guesthouse. Fans of pop music will be familiar with it as the birthplace of ABBA singer Agnetha Fältskog and Cardigans' singer Nina Persson, but Jönköping, whose town charter dates back to 1284, is best known for its modern university. Some 12,000 students—an eighth of its population—today shape the townscape. Surrounded by woodland, Jönköping was, until 1970, the headquarters of Svenska Tändsticks, the global market leader for matches. The Match Museum and the match district by the port pay tribute to this once very important product. The port district with its loft-like brick buildings has evolved into one of the "hip" areas of today.

Astrid Lindgren's Birth Place
(approx. 75 miles/120km)

Emil of Lönneberga, Pippi Longstocking, and the Six Bullerby Children were all created by Astrid Lindgren, and if you want to learn more about this famous Swedish writer of fiction and children's books you will have to take your car on a 75 mile (120km) drive from the guesthouse through Småland to Vimmersby. It was here at the Näs farmstead that Lindgren was born in a red wooden house in 1907. She

Mrs T: "*The house reminds me of my own childhood home, and the views of the lake are simply stunning.*"

had her childhood home remodeled to its original condition in the 1960s, and a visit here is a veritable step back in time. In the Theme park "Astrid Lindgrens World" all her characters come to life – a very popular excursion place for families with kids 5-12 years.

to celebrate

Will you be here in July? Then the Ironman 70.3 triathlon might be something to tempt you! It happens once a year in Jönköping, a 1.18 mile (1.9km) swimming race over the lake, a 13.11 mile (21.1km) run through the city, and a 56 mile (90km) overland bike race. But it's just as much fun—or more?—to simply watch the athletes master their Herculean task.

Ironman 70.3 Jönköping
www.ironman.com/
triathlon/events
July

↑ Nature and the Japanese bath form a harmonious unit that has a wonderfully beneficial effect on body and mind.

YASURAGI
Saltsjö-Boo/Stockholm, Sweden

The Yasuragi Hotel near Stockholm offers the finest in Japanese bathing culture, combined with a comprehensive wellness concept and personal service in a peaceful environment.

hotel info:

Yasuragi
Hamndalsvägen 6
S-132 39 Saltsjö-Boo
Tel.: +46 8 7476400
Mail: info@yasuragi.se
Web: www.yasuragi.se

charging facilities:

14 Type 2 sockets
(a charging cable can
be borrowed from the
hotel)

Located near Stockholm's skerry landscape, the Yasuragi is a wellness hotel you would hardly expect to see in Sweden—because it is authentically Japanese! The name *yasuragi* roughly translates as that deep exhale you do when truly relaxed, something that guests definitely will do at Yasuragi. This is due in part to the minimalist design, which anyone familiar with Japan will immediately recognize as genuine. The owners have adopted an impressive sustainability concept, and the atmosphere here is casual and informal. The rooms feature warm wooden tones, and are stylishly appointed in keeping with the traditional sleeping quarters found in Japan with futons, small seating corners, and dressing areas. Silk paravents in front of the windows create diffused lighting, and once moved aside, guests can enjoy views of the water and skerry landscape. To ensure their everyday stresses are quickly forgotten, all guests receive a traditional *yukata*, a cotton robe to wear around the house during their stay. The yukata is adorned with the traditional Japanese pattern Asanoha.

Japanese bathing culture

The only time you will take your *yukata* off is when you visit the Japanese bath, where you are given a detailed introduction to the Japanese washing ritual—in Japan, the body is first thoroughly washed before you take the actual bath; these are two separate rituals. Only then are you ready for a relaxed session in the *onsen* (hot spring) or sauna. The wellness area with hot springs inside and out in nature as well as different types of saunas and zenmeditation, yoga and treatments for body and face will cover your needs for relaxation. To add to your sense of total peace, no digital devices of any kind are permitted. A day of rest and rejuvenation at Yasuragi is rounded off with a visit to the Saishoku restaurant, where Japanese dishes are prepared using organic local ingredients. The restaurant specializes in vegan and raw food. Alternatively, you can dine at one of the two other restaurants—Teppanyaki and À La Carte, or check out the Sake Bar.

> *Mrs T: "The Yasuragi offers a fantastic journey of wellness and total relaxation. After just one day we were as relaxed as after a week."*

↑ Japanese furnishing culture also defines the decor of the rooms, with paper sliding screens and classic futon bedding.

Insight Yasuragi

Have you ever longed for things to change? In order to make a profound transformation we often need time to look within ourselves and make room for reflection with others. At the Yasuragi, you will be given the tools to help you find that place where insights, creativity and empathy can thrive. Yasuragi has created a strong position by offering a concept that takes the whole human being in consideration. Through its holistic business idea Yasuragi has what it takes to provide both more effective meetings and more creative employees. By calming the nervous system, we get more well-reasoned and make better long-term decisions.

↑ Urban, modern Japan determines the style of the meeting rooms, while the traditional Japanese Asanoha "hemp leaf" pattern can be seen on the yukata gown.

The meeting rooms reflect the hip modernity style of present-day Japan. ↑

AROUND STOCKHOLM
Sweden

Where royalty meets metropolis

Stockholm was built on 14 islands connected by 57 bridges, and is regarded as the most beautiful city in Scandinavia. It is at its best in summer boasting over 18 hours of daylight during June, when locals and visitors take advantage of the long, lazy evenings.

Stockholm
(approx. 12 miles/19km)

Stockholm is Sweden's capital and home to nearly one million people, making it the heart of the nation and also the largest city in Scandinavia. It stretches across fourteen islands at the point where Lake Mälaren opens out into the Baltic Sea, and is marked by an abundance of water and greenery. *Gamla stan*, the largely car-free historic center on the city island of Stadsholmen, is perfect for a relaxed stroll through the town. Here, medieval lanes are home to palaces, dating back to the 17th century, when Sweden ranked as a major power in Europe. Also in the center are Stockholm's cathedral Storkyrkan and the Royal Palace. From the palace, you can see beyond the little island of Helgeandsholmen to Norrmalm district, the 1950s and 1960s new town. Djurgården peninsula, with the Gröna Lund amusement park, is always worth a detour.

Vasa Museum (approx. 13 miles/21km)

The Vasa Museum, or Vasamuseet, on Djurgården is Scandinavia's most visited museum.

It houses the Galone Vasa, which was built to be one of the strongest warships of its day, but which sank after facing the first major wind gust on its maiden voyage in 1628, having sailed just 1,422yds (1,300m). The second canon deck, which had been added after construction began, had made the ship too

Mr T: "Battery-charging here is totally sustainable. The hotel relies on 100 percent renewable energy."

top-heavy for its narrow hull, and even the slightest inclined position enabled water to enter through the canon holes. The wreck was found over 300 years later, and was recovered between 1959 and 1961. As it was very well preserved, 98% of the hull you see today is original. A smaller model next to it, along with other objects and info panels, bring to life the history of the Vasa and Sweden during the Thirty Years' War between 1618 and 1648.

Stockholm's skerry garden
(approx. 3 miles/5km)

Some 24,000 islands of varying sizes, known as skerries, make up Stockholm's skerry garden, which extends about 37 miles (60km)

to celebrate

One of the most characteristic and beloved Swedish traditions of all is Midsummer's Eve. It is always celebrated on the Saturday between June 20 and 26, a day when the sun does not set and the sky never darkens. Traditional dishes such as soused herring, new potatoes with dill, and gravlax are enjoyed with a glass of aquavit and locals make floral crowns to celebrate this longest day of the year. Dancing until dawn is also on the menu, for the next winter is only round the corner.

Midsummer
June 20 to 26

eastward from the city out into the Baltic Sea. It is roughly the same distance north to the island of Vaddö, and south to the skerry known as Öja. The typical flat shape of the skerries is a leftover from the last ice ages, when glaciers wore away the cliffs. Today, the skerries are a popular recreation area for Stockholmers to spend weekends or summer vacations, as evidenced by the numerous jetties and colorful wooden houses you see when taking a ride on a ferry or sailboat.

Tyresta National Park
(approx. 22 miles/ 36km)

Tyresta National Park lies 15½ miles (25km) south of Stockholm, and is best explored from the village of Tyresta, which is easily accessed from Stockholm by bus. The national park, covering an area of 4,942 acres (2,000ha), is crossed by numerous signposted tracks and footpaths, several of which are suitable for beginners. The landscape here is dominated by primeval woodlands with fig trees and mature pines up to 400 years old, as well as lichen-covered cliffs, and picture-postcard lakes, such as Bylsjön and Årsjön. These are interspersed with barren expanses of swamps and moors, while the area west of Lake Stensjön is only slowly recovering after a major wildfire in 1999.

Uppsala
(approx. 58 miles/93km)

Sweden's fourth largest city, with a population of around 15,000, is located a good one-hour's drive north of the hotel. The journey will take you through the densely wooded landscape of central Sweden. Uppsala is home to a university that was founded as early as 1477, and so it is not surprising to find it very much a student town. The Gothic cathedral next to the university is the largest church in Scandinavia, while the Palace on the hillside dominates the entire city. Lovers of exotic plants will enjoy a visit to the Botanical Garden in the Palace

↑ A view of the old town of Stockholm, resplendent with its Royal Palace on the right and Stockholm's main church, the Storkyrkan, in a slightly elevated position to the left.

↑ Most of the skerry islands are small and uninhabited, others often just have a few houses and of course a jetty; together they make up an ideal recreational area for the city dwellers from Stockholm. Those who like to be active rather than seeking solitude can visit the larger, inhabited islands, such as Sandhamn, Blidö, and Utö, where there are hotels, restaurants, and marinas, as well as many recreational facilities.

grounds, as well as the former garden of Carl Linnaeus, the founder of the modern system of naming organisms in botany and zoology, who died in Uppsala.

COPPERHILL MOUNTAIN LODGE
Åre, Sweden

The Copperhill Mountain Lodge, located in the famous Swedish ski resort of Åre, is a magical design hotel that lives up to its name, featuring numerous copper elements in its interior.

hotel info:

Copperhill Mountain Lodge
Åre Björnen
S-837 97 Åre
Tel.: +46 647 14300
Mail: info@copperhill.se
Web: www.copperhill.se

charging facilities:

1 Tesla DeC (Tesla only)
1 Tesla DeC (all EVs)

The approach to the Swedish ski resort of Åre and the Copperhill Mountain Lodge leads through the remote vastness of central Sweden, dotted with many of the legendary "Beware of the moose" roadsigns. The imposing, modern hotel sits on top of a mountain, right by the ski slope, and its multi-story lobby with a 72ft (22m) ceiling height boasts a large open fireplace and a giant copper wall that pays homage to the area's copper mining history. Other natural materials, such as pine and slate, work with warm, modern design elements to create a spectacular contemporary classic. The lobby, much like the rooms and suites, is a mix of designer statement and

> Mr T: *"The hotel spa is open from 6 a.m., so we usually manage to do a few lengths in the pool or sweat it out in the sauna before breakfast."*

"hygge." The Copperhill Mountain Lodge also features a superbly equipped spa area, and when the winter weather is not conducive to outdoor activities, or after a morning on the slopes, you can head straight to the indoor swimming pool, the heated outdoor pool, or the sauna and enjoy a massage or beauty treatments. Alternatively, take a seat at the stylish bar or enjoy local fish, meat, mushrooms, and berries in the restaurant.

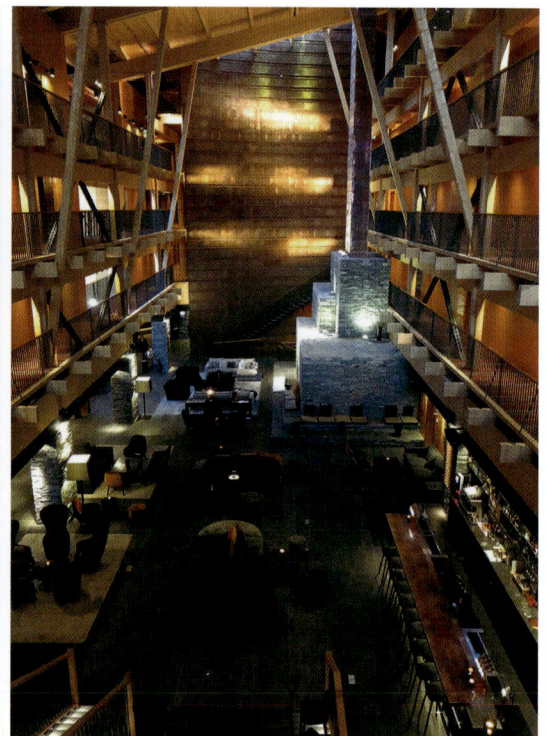

AROUND ÅRE
Sweden

Where Sweden goes skiing

The mountains around Åre are among Sweden's oldest and most popular ski resorts. The World Ski Championships have taken place in Åre in 1954, 2007, and most recently in 2019 and the Ski World Cup is also regularly hosted here. But the area is just as stunning in summer, when you can spot reindeer, elk, bears, and the king of the forest, the mighty moose.

Storsjön
(approx. 34 miles/55km)

Trångsviken by Lake Storsjön is a good hour's drive east of the hotel. Sweden's fifth largest lake measures 176sq miles (456sq km) in area, and is up to 243ft (74m) deep. The lake is great for swimming (popular with hardy local people but maybe a little cold for visitors), fishing, and kayaking. Be sure to summon all your courage if you're tempted to swim in the chilly waters—local legend has it that the Storsjöodjudet, a snake-like sea monster with a dog-shaped head, lives at the bottom of the Storsjön. The Jamtli Museum (see Östersund) has a small exhibition dedicated to the creature. Who knows, you might catch a glimpse of it from the safety of the shore as you drive along the scenic, 84 mile (135km) route around the lake past Östersund, Frösön, Orrviken, and Myrviken.

Östersund (approx. 61 miles/98km)

Östersund, with a population of around 50,000, forms the heart of the Jämtland region. Founded as late as the 18th century, and laid out in checkerboard style, the city is rich in green spaces. It is also a major transport hub. Along the Prästgatan ("the priest's street") you will find interesting shops worth browsing, while the neighboring Storgatan ("main street"), features many picturesque old townhouses. Anyone wanting to immerse

Mrs T: "*As a Tesla driver, you are allotted a place in the heated underground car park, very convenient in sub-zero temperatures.*"

themselves farther into Jämtland's history can head to the Jämtli, a fascinating local history museum with permanent and temporary exhibitions, and a large open-air section on Lake Storsjön. Art enthusiasts will be sure to find interesting souvenirs and works of art at one of more than twenty galleries.

to celebrate

The Storsjöyran Festival, aka The Great Lake Festival, has been taking place in the city center of Östersund since 1983. Around 35,000 to 40,000 visitors arrive each year, making the festival one of the largest in Sweden. Past star billings have included rock and pop greats such as Bryan Adams, The Pretenders, Iggy Pop, Motörhead, B.B. King and the Pet Shop Boys.

Storsjöyran Festival
Östersund
www. yran.se
July or August

ANGVIK GAMLE HANDELSSTED
Angvik, Norway

The Angvik Gamle Handelssted at Tingvollfjord is an idyllic "trading city" with a lively cultural heritage where exclusivity and high quality combine perfectly, creating an informal family atmosphere.

hotel info:

Angvik Gamle
Handelssted
Kjøpmannsgata
N-6636 Angvik
Tel.: +47 71 291300
Mail: post@
angvik-hotell.no
Web: www.
classicnorway.no/
hotell/angvik-gamle-
handelssted

charging facilities:

2 Tesla DeC (Tesla only)
1 Tesla DeC (all EVs)

Situated on the tranquil western shores of the Tinvollfjord, the white buildings of Angvik Gamle Handelssted with their bright red roofs stand out like beacons, visible from some distance away. This meticulously restored boutique hotel is run by the Angvik (pronounced Angvikja) family, who can look back on a long mercantile history. The rooms at Angvik Gamle Handelssted are exceptionally warm and luxurious, and the comforters are divine!—making the hotel the perfect base for excursions into the surrounding fjord landscape, and also an ideal haven when the Norwegian weather prevents you from stepping outside. On chilly days, head to the hotel's small but sophisticated spa, or investigate the on-site museum and learn about the Angvik family's history. The hotel places great emphasis on authentic local cuisine, which is heavily fish-based. Guests can also hire fishing equipment and a rowboat and catch their own fish in the fjord. If you prefer exploring the surroundings closer to the hotel, simply hire a bike. The evenings are best spent by the crackling log fire in the living room.

> *Mr T: "The package of perfectly matched wines to accompany the five-course evening meal is presented with passion and confidence by the friendly waiter."*

AROUND ANGVIK
Norway

Spectacular roads in spectacular scenery

The fjords often resemble elongated lakes, and the climate on the shores is mostly mild thanks to the Gulf Stream. If, however, the weather becomes stormy, the scenery is best enjoyed from the safety of your car as the strong winds create huge waves in the fjord, providing a fascinating natural spectacle.

Atlantic Ocean Road (approx. 53 miles/85km)

A very scenic excursion from Angvik Gamle Handelssted takes you to the open seas along the Atlantic Ocean Road, a section of Highway 64 between the towns of Vevang and Karvag. The road is one of the most impressive in the world, initially snaking through wild landscapes, before heading past a series of tiny islands to the rugged costal stretch. With some sections running barely above the surface of the Norwegian Sea, and others crossing surreally bent bridges at heights of 100ft (30m), making them seem more like roller coasters than roadway bridges, the Atlantic Ocean Road unlocks new vistas and perspectives at every turn. Even—or perhaps especially!—in bad weather, when the waves lash the shore, it certainly makes for a unique setting.

Tingvollfjord (approx. ½ mile/1km)

Looking out over the Tingvollfjord from the hotel on clear days, you can see the small town of Tingvoll about 4½ miles (7km) away on the far shore. In most parts, however,

Tingvollfjord is a mere 2 miles (3km) wide; north to south, on the other hand, the inlet measures about 32 miles (52km) long, from the islands of Bergsøy and Aspøy, with the last 10 miles (17km) from the Ballsnes headland onward forming part of the Sunndalsfjord.

Mrs T: "The beautifully designed museum brings to life the story of the Angvik family, who engaged in lively trade in the town."

Near Angvik, on the western side, you can follow waterside Highways 666 and 62 southeast to the start of the fjord in Sunndalsøra, where you change to National Road 70. This road will take you back northwest, past Tingvoll, and on to the islands of Aspøy and Bergsøy at the end of the fjord.

↑ Driving along the Atlantic Ocean Road battered by the waves from a stormy sea is unforgettable!

↑ You can enjoy some quiet and restful moments at the Storfjord Hotel. Its warmth and cozy furnishings keep even the harshest of the Scandinavian winters at bay.

STORFJORD HOTEL
Skodje, Norway

The Storfjord Hotel is a luxury log cabin-style boutique hotel, located in a fantastic location above a fjord, which makes the house an absolute must on any visit to Norway.

hotel info:

Storfjord Hotel
Øvre Glomset
N-6260 Skodje
Tel.: +47 70 274922
Mail: info@
storfjordhotel.com
Web: www.
storfjordhotel.com

charging facilities:

2 Tesla DeC (Tesla only)
1 Tesla DeC (all EVs)
1 CEE 16 A
3-phase (all EVs)

The approach to the Storfjord Hotel is an experience in itself, for the property benefits from a stunning hilltop location, with panoramic views extending over the Storfjord. The top-quality chalet architecture exudes such a great sense of tranquility that guests instantly feel the stress of everyday life melt away. The elegant rooms and suites are spread over several log cabins which feature the typically Norwegian turf roofs. Equipped with four-poster beds, fireplaces, seating areas, and large windows, they lack nothing in the way of comfort. What makes the Storfjord Hotel a truly unique place in Norway is the combination of rustic chic, in the form of the solid, hand-crafted log walls, with works of art and antiques as well as the highest quality materials and modern design. The hotel's various common areas are so inviting, you can make yourself at home here by the fire with a drink or a book whenever you wish. The small spa area, with its sauna and bubbling Jacuzzi, will similarly nourish your body and mind. And to cap it all off, enjoy an exquisite dinner in a wonderfully romantic setting overlooking the splendid panorama of the fjord and the surrounding mountains. The Storfjord Hotel is perfectly equipped in this department, serving the best local cuisine using fresh ingredients sourced from local producers. The hotel particularly prides itself on its vast selection of regional cheeses and the Storfjordbrygg—a home-brewed ale that is only available at the hotel. There are many activities available close to the hotel, ranging from fishing, kayaking, and hiking to skiing in winter.

> *Mr T:* *"Whatever the weather, you'll feel like jogging through the woods. The air is so pure, your batteries will be charged straightaway."*

↑ Three Destination Charger provide "food" for your car—and the electricity is provided in an ecological fashion, too, through hydropower.

Connecting with nature

The Storfjord Hotel always conveys a sense of being at one with nature. As such, it is a deeply restful experience to sit on its terrace with a cup of hot coffee, and take in the greenery of the trees and the blues of the sky and fjord. It is worth pointing out here that Norway generates most of its electricity through hydropower, which means your Tesla will be constantly charged at one of the three property's Destination Charger.

Insight Storfjord Hotel

Slowing down is the principal motto at the Storfjord Hotel. The hotel lies in a green, secluded, wooded hillside with a panoramic view of the Storfjord, and so it is easy to switch off and take in the wonderful scenery. Grass-covered rooftops and the handcrafted wood of the log cabins connects the guests with the hotel's natural surroundings. The rooms are spacious and very comfortable, and the hotel even boasts a magnificent four-poster bed made of wood, in which guests can sleep soundly and deeply and wake up refreshed and free from the stress of their everyday lives.

↑ You simply have to feel in harmony with nature as you dine in the grass-roofed main house by the open fireplace, or relax in your log cabin room, gazing dreamily at the log fire and the Scandinavian forest.

The Storfjord Hotel lies in the middle of Norway's fjord country, right on the fjord through which the Hurtigruten mail boats ↑ and summer cruise ships pass, as they head for the famous Geirangerfjord.

AROUND SKODJE
Norway

The fjords of Norway

Perhaps the most beautiful sights in Norway are its fjords, and the most attractive of those are to be found near Ålesund, including the legendary Geirangerfjord. Even if you don't have a fixed destination in mind though, a ride through this unique countryside is one of the most perfect travel experiences.

Storfjord
(approx. ½ mile/1km)

The hotel overlooks the Storfjord, which runs through a good part of Møre og Romsdal province. At its Norwegian Sea end, the Storfjord becomes the Sulafjord, a sound between relatively flat islands; further inland, the fjord is narrower, and the mountains on both sides are steeper and higher. The Storfjord has several side-fjords and at its deepest point it measures 2,228ft (679m). It ends near the village of Stranda, where it becomes the Norddalsfjord continuing to the east and the Sunnylvsfjord, which runs southward. From this latter section, the famous Geirangerfjord branches off a few miles along.

Ålesund
(approx. 19¼ miles/31km)

The journey west to Ålesund takes a good half hour. The port city is a stop point for the Hurtigruten, the former Norwegian mail boats and today a popular cruise ship line. The town extends over several islands, the two forming the city center separated by the stretch of

water from which the town gained its name. It is the inner city that makes Ålesund unique. During a major fire in 1904, all the wooden structures were burned down. The town was rebuilt in stone, with a little private help from German Emperor Wilhelm II, and designed in the Art Nouveau style popular at the time.

Mrs T: "Here you can quickly find peace—and bliss is perfect if you also happen upon a rainbow above the green forest!"

Later changes made to these buildings have now mostly been reversed again, and when strolling through the city today you'll feel yourself transported a good 100 years back in time. From the viewpoint on Aksla Mountain, which rises in the city park, you can enjoy fabulous views of Ålesund and the sea. And as to what's going on beneath the sea's surface — that's best discovered in the Atlantic Sea-Park, Ålesund's excellent aquarium.

Art Nouveau Center Swan Pharmacy
(approx. 19¼ miles/31km)

The former Swan Pharmacy (Svaneapotek) in the city center is an outstanding example of the city's reconstruction after 1904 in the Art

Nouveau style. The building was designed by the architect Hagbarth Martin Schytte-Berg for the pharmacist and local councillor Jørgen Anton Øwre, who lived above the pharmacy. The granite stone building, which is adorned with a tower, gables, and an oriel window, is inspired by Romanesque architecture as well as Norwegian stave churches, and is now a listed building. You can visit the pharmacy and the original living quarters, and learn all about the fire and the reconstruction of Ålesund. The Center hosts temporary and permanent Art Nouveau exhbitions.

Høgkubben (approx. 10 miles/16km)

If you don't want to go jogging or hiking right outside the hotel, then Høgkubben, which lies in the direction of Myrland, is an attractive destination. The mountain top can be reached from Myrland, Blindheim, or Spjelkavik in a one-hour hike which is suitable for beginners wearing sturdy shoes. On reaching the flat top, at 1,148ft (350m) altitude, you can picnic in peace and, above all, enjoy the fantastic views of the three starting places, the Storfjord, and the steeply rising mountains beyond, as well as of Ålesund and the open sea in the distance.

Ørnesvingen via the Geirangerfjord (approx. 47 miles/75km)

Covering the distance from the hotel to the main fjord area can be an all-day affair, yet well worth the time and effort. The stunning route to the Ørnesvingen Viewpoint will make you feel happy that you are driving in an emission-free and quiet electric car. For long stretches, the road runs beside the majestic Storfjord and then, after crossing it by ferry, you continue on the Ørnesvegen ("eagles' road"), which is up to 10% steep in some parts. Eventually you reach the topmost of eleven hairpin bends, the Ørnesvingen ("eagles' bend"). The view hundreds of yards down into the Geirangerfjord is simply

↑ The Art Nouveau jewel of Ålesund is in a unique location, spread over several islands on the Norwegian coast. The city is a stop-over point for the Hurtigruten cruise line as well as a starting point for trips into Norway's beautiful fjord landscapes.

↑ The UNESCO World Heritage Site of Geirangerfjord is used by cruise ships only in the summer, because avalanches are possible in winter and could cause high waves. The most beautiful view is from the hills around.

breathtaking. Geiranger town itself and the huge, white cruise liners in the fjord look like tiny toys from up here. It is also impressive how the nearby waterfall has been integrated into the viewing area, making this an especially delightful place.

AUSTRIA

↑ The two-toque gastronomy of the Heurigenhof offers excellent food and outstanding wines within the cozy ambience of a wine-cellar vault.

HEURIGENHOF BRÜNDLMAYER

Langenlois, Austria

In Lower Austria, the Heurigenhof Bründlmayer in Kamptal is a place where wine connoisseurs and gourmets get their money's worth—a true oasis of relaxation and pleasure.

hotel info:

Heurigenhof
Bründlmayer
Walterstr. 14
A-3550 Langenlois
Tel.: +43 2734 2883
Mail: office@
heurigenhof.at
Web: www.
heurigenhof.at

charging facilities:

1 Tesla DeC (Tesla only)
1 Tesla DeC (all EVs)

In the heart of the wine-growing village of Langenlois in Lower Austria, hidden behind an unremarkable wall, you will find the Heurigenhof Bründlmayer country estate. Guests arrive in the courtyard, which is romantically covered in grapevines. Clustered around the yard are the beautifully renovated main house as well as the hotel's wine cellar and the outstanding restaurant in a vaulted room. The young hosts, Victoria and Martin, have been running the Heurigenhof for ten years, always to the highest standards: professional, charming, with a love for detail and creativity, and with great passion. At the Heurigenhof, you can enjoy excellent food and drinks, as well as the team's warm, personable hospitality. In the morning, a romantic breakfast table awaits you in one of the lovingly designed large rooms. The restaurant's delicious culinary highlights are just as beautifully presented and are, of course, always accompanied by matching wines. A crackling open fire creates a warm, cozy, and relaxed atmosphere, and so do the hosts who will introduce you to the world of white, red, and sparkling wines with their great expertise. The excellent quality of the food is attested to by two Gault Millau chef's toques. From April to September, when the weather permits, you can also enjoy a picnic in the open air, among the vines, roses, and wine barrels. Here you could try, for example, some of the homemade speacialities, such as Bründlmayer's Traubenkern-Brot (grapeseed bread), the local Kamptal Wurzelspeck (smoked ham), or a Bio-Lachsforelle (smoked organic mountain trout).

Mr T: "If you fear you cannot find what you like among the 40 Bründlmayer wines on the list, the cellar also has 400 wines from around the world!"

↑ Contemporary luxuries and antiques combine to create a charming ambience in the three guest rooms.

Three exquisite guest rooms

The three charming guest rooms, each one a jewel in itself, are arranged around the courtyard. Furnished to the highest standard, the rooms combine the best of modern Austrian design with selected vintage items. The comfortable box spring beds guarantee a relaxing night's sleep. Fully recharged in the morning, you can take your "vintner's breakfast" whenever you wake up, together with a fragrant cup from your own espresso machine.

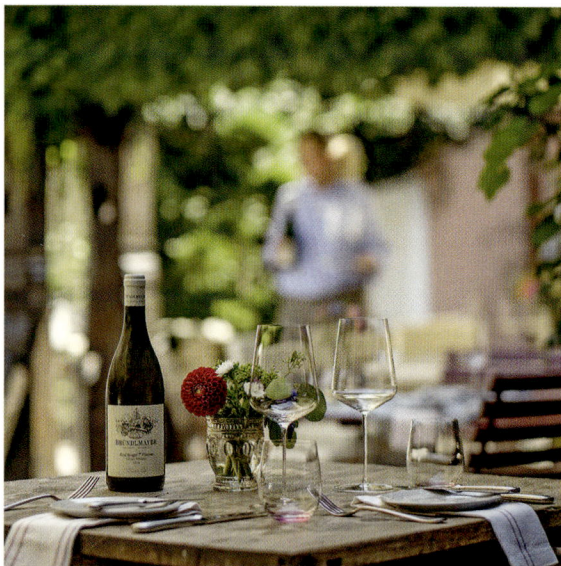

Insight Heurigenhof Bründlmayer

The excellent wines of the Bründlmayer vineyard, which, together with the Heurigenhof hotel, forms a part of the wine estate, are another highlight. The special local geographic and geological conditions are the perfect basis for growing the grapes to make characterful, rounded white wines. The hills of the Waldviertel protect the vineyards from the north-westerly winds. Stony soils store the sun's heat during the day, to release it slowly at night, when it cools down significantly. You can sample the fine wines on a visit to the impressive wine cellar, but the wines taste best when accompanying the restaurant's tasting menu—and later at home once you've stocked up.

↑ The spacious apartments are so comfortable that you may like to spend a whole day there, relaxing while reading a book, for example. Bründlmayer's homemade foods have an excellent reputation. In fine weather, you can enjoy them in the arbor.

AROUND LANGENLOIS
Austria

At the heart of Austrian wine culture

The Kamptal climate, characterized by warm summer days and cool nights, followed by a long-lasting, sunny fall, offers the ideal conditions for full-bodied white wines, bursting with fruitiness and character—just like the ones produced by the Bründlmayer vineyard.

Rosenburg Castle
(approx. 9 miles/15km)

You reach Schloss Rosenburg, situated above the River Kamp, after a short drive from the hotel. The castle was built as a small Romanesque fortress in around 1150 and was later enlarged in the Gothic style. After 1487, it was transformed into a Renaissance castle. Following extensive repairs, the sprawling complex with its many towers today looks as it did in 1681, when marriage brought it to the Hoyos-Sprinzenstein family, who have been the owners ever since. The interior of the castle can be visited. As well as information on the castle and the family history, the small museum also has an exhibition on falconry, a perfect complement to one of the bird of prey shows, held here every year between April and October.

Krems an der Donau
(approx. 5 miles/8km)

Krems an der Donau is the nearest town. Its old town was inscribed as a UNESCO World Heritage site in 2000, as part of the Wachau Cultural Landscape. The city's landmark is the Steiner Tor (below). The gate's striking main tower with the double-headed eagle is flanked by two symmetrical side towers. At the other end of the old town, the Piaristenkirche reveals in its Gothic structure the influence of the architects of St. Stephen's Cathedral in Vienna.

Mrs T: "I particularly love the various package deals on offer, combining food and accommodation."

The grand high altar dates from the baroque period. Yet Krems is not just historical splendor, it also offers a modern art experience in the Stein district. A visit to the Kunsthalle and the Krems Caricature Museum, as well as to the State Gallery of Lower Austria, which opened in 2019, is highly recommended.

to celebrate

On the outskirts of Langenlois is Haindorf Castle, which has been the venue for the Langenlois Castle Festival since 1996. From the end of July to the middle of August, a popular operetta, such as *The Bird Seller* by Carl Zeller or *The Gipsy Princess* by Emmerich Kálmán, is on the program. During the interval, a glass of the festival wine will add to the summery ambience of the Castle Festival—the winemakers select a festival wine among the regional submissions each year.

Langenlois Castle Festival www.schlossfestspiele.at end July–mid-August

↑ Old and new, tradition and contemporary design are the components skillfully combined by Mark Wiesinger to create this homely and comfortable ambience.

HOTEL & VILLA AUERSPERG

Salzburg, Austria

A notable attention to detail and personal service make the Hotel & Villa Auersperg a charming home away from home—a beautiful owner-run boutique hotel and hideaway in Salzburg.

hotel info:

Hotel & Villa Auersperg
Auerspergstr. 61
A-5020 Salzburg
Tel.: +43 662 88944-0
Mail:
info@auersperg.at
Web:
www.auersperg.at

charging facilities:

2 Tesla DeC (Tesla only)
1 Tesla DeC (all EVs)

If Wolfgang Amadeus Mozart were alive in Salzburg today, he might be one of the creatives from the Andräviertel district where the Hotel & Villa Auersperg is located. He might even enjoy drinking his morning coffee in the A*Bar & Lounge while composing his next piece on his laptop. The stylish room with its huge panoramic window to the garden is a good example of what you can achieve, if, like the hosts Bettina and Mark Wiesinger, you tackle an exceptional hotel project with verve and conviction. Since founding in 1960 by Bettina Wiesinger's grandmother, the hotel and villa complex has gradually been developed over the years. Today Bettina's hotel comprises 55 rooms as well as suites, all of which carry the signature of her husband, who is responsible for the design and lighting and the selection of furniture.

A city retreat with a paradise garden

The integration of the enchanting garden into the overall concept is particularly successful, making the Hotel & Villa Auersperg a small hideaway in the heart of the bustling city. The hotel guests—many of them regulars—always appreciate the Wiesingers' warm hospitality as well as the sustainability of the establishment and its many attractive details. So, for example, you can hear not only the chirping of birds in the garden, but also the buzzing of bees around their hives. The hotel's own honey graces the breakfast table, together with many other home-produced delicacies and foods sourced from local organic suppliers in Salzburg. The rooms are equipped with a selection of books and magazines as well as top-of-the-range audio systems for their guests' comfort and entertainment. And, naturally, the hotel also boasts a comfortable, flower-decked roof terrace from where you can enjoy fabulous views across the city of Salzburg after a relaxing visit to the hotel's sauna. A few floors below, meanwhile, your Tesla is recharging at one of the three destination chargers, which Mr and Mrs Wiesinger have installed at their hotel.

> **Mrs T:** *"The morning yoga class in the small but fine spa over the roofs of Salzburg did me the world of good!"*

↑ The mixture of design classics and bold, modern designs convinces with its easy elegance and lightness.

↑ The garden was created with great attention to detail. It invites you to relax surrounded by nature. The colorful flower beds are not only a feast for the eyes, but also attract bees and other insects.

Insight Hotel & Villa Auersperg

Bettina and Mark Wiesinger are the third generation to run the city retreat Hotel & Villa Auersperg. Over the years, the entire complex has grown steadily to reach its present size. Old and new are skillfully combined here, but above all, it is the tasteful interior design that sets the hotel apart from its competitors. Creative lighting effects, bold and daring, but always stylish, and clever color combinations complement the contemporary and antique furniture. Only fabrics and materials of the best and sustainably produced quality are used.

The design plays perfectly with lights and lighting. Books, magazines, and audio systems in the rooms ↑ make you feel at ease, relaxed, and at home.

AROUND SALZBURG
Austria

A dreamlike setting for everyone

Salzburg is unique. The amount of culture, magnificent architecture and sheer joy of life that prevail here in this medium-sized town, is hard to find anywhere else. In addition, the surrounding Alpine panorama offers an enchanting scenery—reason enough to explore the area in a climate-friendly way, on foot.

to celebrate

The Salzburg Festival, which takes place every summer, is undoubtedly one of the best-known art festivals in the world, dedicated to theater, opera, and concerts. Traditionally, an open-air performance of The Play of the Everyman by Hugo von Hofmannsthal on cathedral square is always on the program. Other operas top-class concerts are staged at venues next to the cathedral square: the House for Mozart, the Felsenreitschule, and the Grossee Festspielhaus (Large Festival Hall).

Salzburger Festspiele
www.salzburger
festspiele.at
July–August

Hohensalzburg Castle
(1.2 miles/2km)

Salzburg's famous landmark is the Hohensalzburg Castle, visible from afar, on the fortress hill above the historic center. The complex, built to protect the independent Archbishopric of Salzburg from attacks, dates back to a small castle built in 1077 and was extended up to the time of the Thirty Years' War. The extensive bastions, which surround the main castle and shape the fortress today were only built from 1633 to 1645. Salzburg was integrated into Austria in 1805, and in 1861 the fortress function was abolished. A visit to Europe's largest fully preserved castle includes the Prince's Chambers, Salt Magazine, Salzburg Puppet Museum, and the Museum of the K.u.k. Infantry Regiment "Erzherzog Rainer" Regiment No. 59.

Mozart's Birthplace
(approx. ½ mile/1km)

While Getreidegasse 9 may be a rather mundane address, it is the destination of virtually all visitors to Salzburg, since Wolfgang Amadeus Mozart was born here on January 27, 1756.

The city's most famous son, celebrated as a wunderkind musician and composer, spent his childhood and youth in the yellow building, which now houses a museum. Visitors will see a reconstructed bourgeois apartment from the 18th century as it might have been inhabited by the Mozart family. Also

Mr T: "It's great that the hotel is committed to the common good and ensures a healthy life-work balance for the team."

presented here are numerous original documents, letters, and memorabilia of Mozart's life in Salzburg, not least his children's violin and a clavichord. Each year, changing exhibitions offer additional interesting insights even to the best-informed Mozart fans.

Mirabell Palace
(approx. ½ mile/1km)

Mirabell Palace was erected in the town's historic center in 1606 by Prince-Archbishop Wolf Dietrich von Raitenau, who had it built for his mistress, Salome Alt. If love was the key theme for the whole castle, today it is found especially in the Marble Hall, which is considered one of the most beautiful wedding venues in the world. The hall is also used for concerts, and as one enters it via the "Engelstreppe" (angels' staircase) lined by putti, it does not take much imagination to see father Leopold Mozart and his children Wolfgang Amadeus and Nannerl, who performed here more than 250 years ago. Outside, the Mirabell garden in front of the castle was built in 1690 and is still recognizable as a baroque geometric garden. Its axis is visually perfectly in line with the Cathedral and Hohensalzburg Castle.

Museum of Modern Art
(approx. 1¼ miles/2 km)

The Salzburg Museum of Modern Art presents its exhibitions at two locations—at the early baroque Rupertinum in the historic center and in the futuristic new building and study center on the Mönchsberg. The spectrum ranges from classic modernism via conceptual art and light installations to audiovisual media. The museum also holds the national collection of Austrian photography after 1945, and is now officially known as the Austrian Federal Photo Collection. A recent focus is on works by non-European artists and—since 2014, on permanent loan—exhibits from the collection of the Generali Foundation.

Salzburg Cathedral
(approx. ½ mile/1km)

As part of the historic center of the city, Salzburg Cathedral is a UNESCO World Heritage site and the cathedral of the Roman Catholic Archdiocese of Salzburg. The first building was completed in 774 but succumbed to fire. Work on the building we see today, the third building in this place, began in 1614, culminating in 1628. While the west façade of Untersberger marble—a light limestone—stands out with its decorative figures and the two 266ft (81m) high towers, the rest of the façade was kept plain. Inside the three-aisled

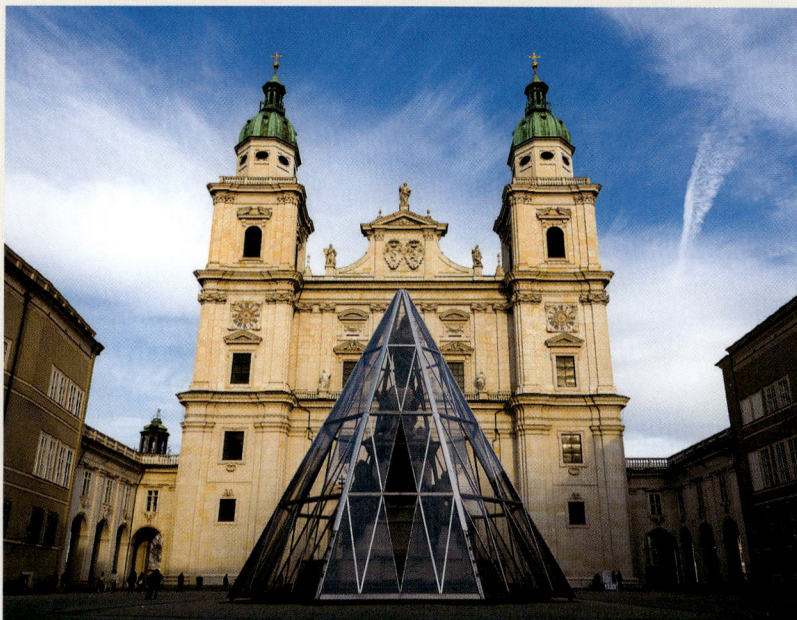

↑ The statue of the Virgin in front of the cathedral, which is protected in a glass pyramid, dates from the second half of the 18th century. The cathedral itself was built almost 150 years earlier, as the first early baroque church north of the Alps.

↑ Not only wedding couples and their guests are enchanted by the romantic beauty of the Mirabell Palace's baroque park with its beautifully kept geometric borders, its fountain, and its many sculptures—including those in the Zwerglgarten (Dwarf Garden).

cathedral, the entire splendor of the architectural style is again to be admired, culminating in the crossing with its organs and the 233ft (71m) high dome, featuring frescoes from the Old Testament.

↑ Modern accents do not bely the age-old traditions of this alpine family business. Whether the enjoyment of sheer luxury, relaxed well-being and fine cuisine is more fun in summer or winter, guests will have to decide for themselves!

HOTEL MOHR LIFE RESORT

Lermoos, Austria

Its modern alpine style and a large spa area with views of the Zugspitze, Germany's highest peak, turn a stay at the family-run Hotel MOHR life resort into an unforgettable experience.

hotel info:

Hotel MOHR life resort
GmbH + Co. KG
Innsbrucker Str. 40
A-6631 Lermoos/Tirol
Tel.: +43 5673 2362
Mail: willkommen@
mohr-life-resort.at
Web: www.mohr-life-
resort.at

charging facilities:

1 Tesla DeC (Tesla only)
1 Tesla DeC (all EVs)
8 Tesla SuC (Tesla only)

A hotel with its own small museum—that must be rather an unusual find! Nor are there probably many establishments outside of the larger cities that can look back on more than 210 years of hotel history—and enjoy a view of the Zugspitze that has remained unobstructed until the present day. What began as an inn in Lermoos in 1806 has over the generations developed into a 4-star luxury hotel: the Hotel MOHR life resort. Still family-run, it combines modern alpine style on the outside with a design-oriented feel-good atmosphere inside, without ever losing sight of

its origins. Warm wooden tones predominate in the light rooms and suites, ranging from comfortable double rooms to the airy penthouse with an open fireplace or the Arabic-inspired garden spa suite with its large private terrace. But as the saying goes: "There is no rule without exception!" The new 007 suite is the only one that is hi-tech, with design classics in the Bauhaus style. And the lounge area of this suite is the only place to boast a large panoramic window, beyond which you can see—as if in a James Bond film—your own (electric) car in a private section of the underground car park!

Mr T: "The hotel's fantastically extensive spa and leisure program and facilities do not really leave much time to explore the surroundings."

Optimal relaxation

The ultramodern ambience of the 007 suite is repeated in the cubic architecture of the MOHR escape, which was opened as recently as November 2018. Adjoining the main building, this adults-only spa and wellness area is styled in exposed concrete, which, in conjunction with its large infinity pool and the fabulous Zugspitze views, creates its own special ambience. Relax Lounges, a sauna area, and a variety of wellness programs guarantee optimal relaxation. To complement the overall experience with culinary pleasure, the motto at the MOHR life resort's restaurant is "Anything but bland!" The hotel's cuisine presents a menu featuring a mix of Tyrolean and Mediterranean specialties as well as crossover dishes, which you can enjoy—once again—while admiring the panoramic views of the Zugspitze summit.

↑ The Zugspitze massif dominates the vast plateau where Lermoos and the neighboring municipality of Ehrwald are located.

↑ The panoramic indoor pool offers fantastic views of the surrounding alpine mountainscape, yet it is so beautiful itself that the interior is just as lovely to behold.

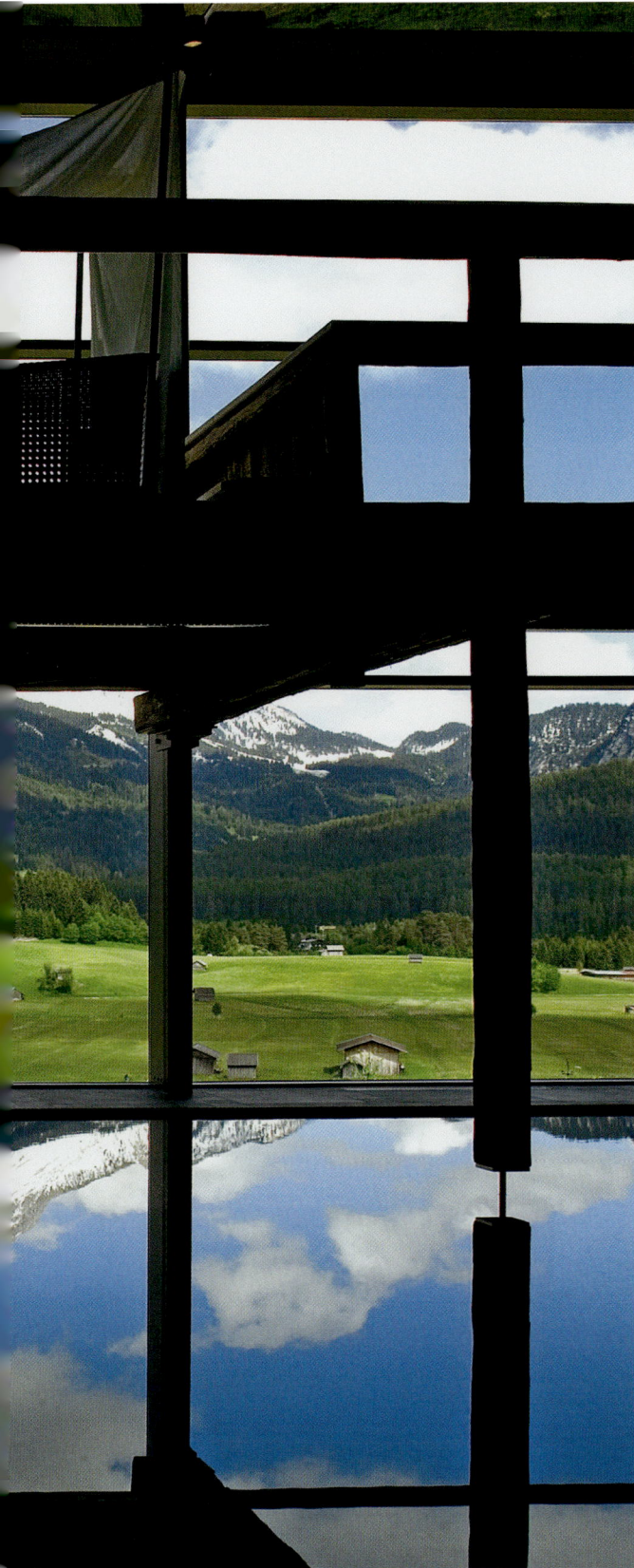

The hotel's extensive offer of accommodation ranges from generously sized double rooms to luxurious suites with ↑ panoramic bathtub or fireplace.

↑ The MOHR escape is a light-flooded, see-through concrete structure housing the exclusive new spa facilities of the hotel, with an outdoor pool right outside the building granting overwhelming views of the mountains.

Insight Hotel MOHR life resort

With the introduction of the MOHR escape, the hotel, which is highly respected as a wellness center, has significantly increased its recreational and relaxation area. Modern architecture blends perfectly into the landscape, and a generously sized indoor and a huge outdoor pool create a space entirely dedicated to tranquility and self-discovery. In the escape building, 26 multi-sensor room installations provide an atmosphere that is entirely dedicated to guests' immediate needs, shutting out all the cares and worries of everyday life. At MOHR escape, guests can immerse themselves in space and water, and experience total recuperation.

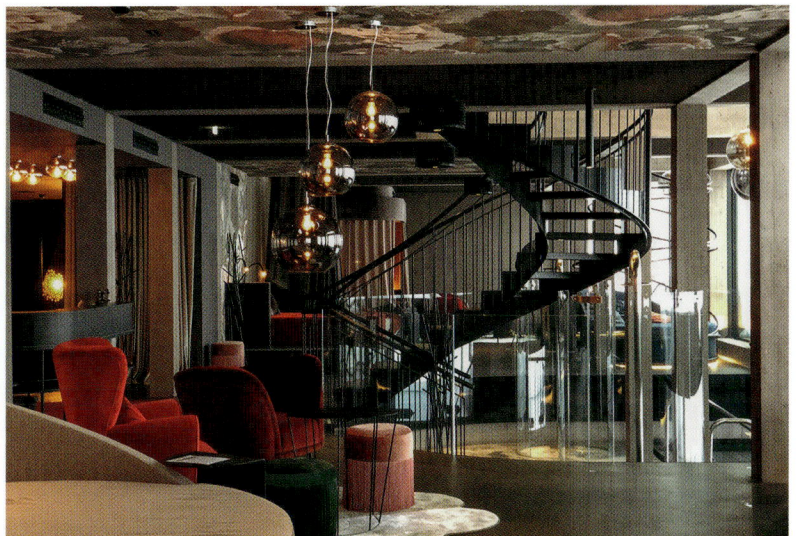

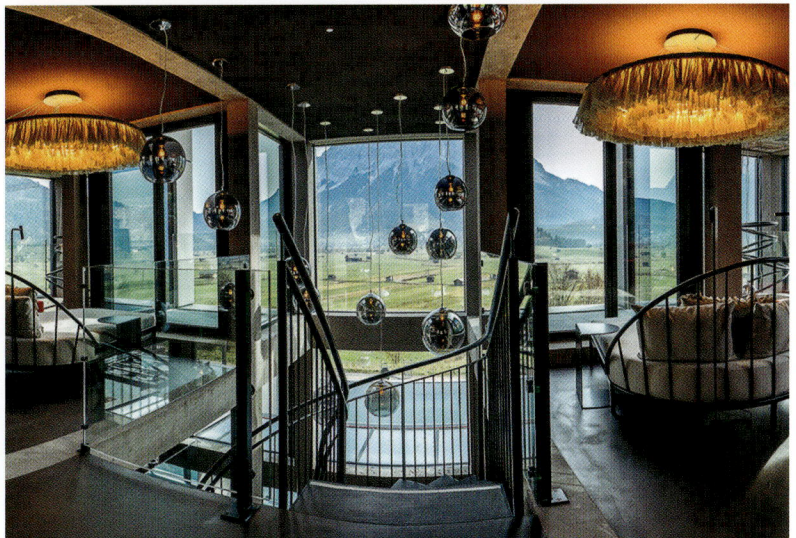

Modern design objects indicate that the hotel is dedicated to the present day. Relaxation at the MOHR escape adds to the ↑ stimulating atmosphere of a truly extravagant and luxurious interior space.

AROUND LERMOOS

Austria

Ever-present views of the Zugspitze

The two communities of Lermoos and Ehrwald are located on a wide plateau at an altitude of some 3,280ft (1,000m) altitude, in a former marshland, directly below the Zugspitze massif. Fairly sure to have snow, this holiday region offers many opportunities for active leisure pursuits in winter and summer.

Grubigstein
(approx. ½ mile/1km)

The Grubigstein is the "local mountain" of Lermoos, with a 7,326ft (2,233m) high summit rising directly to the southwest of the village. In winter, the mountain is a popular ski resort, reached from Lermoos via cable car. It takes you to ski runs of different degrees of difficulty, but also to the Grubighütte alpine hut, directly at the mountain station at 6,726ft (2,050m). Lower down, at 5,751ft (1,753m), is the Wolfratshauser Hütte, a hut operated by the German Alpine Club. In summer, many hikers ascend directly from the valley, and the huts may be their main destination. To continue up to the three-peak summit, you should be sure of foot, as the terrain is rugged—steep, rocky, with grass and scree interspersed.

Seebensee
(approx. 4½ miles/7km)

You've packed your hiking boots? Great, then there's nothing in the way of a tour to the Seebensee. This small mountain lake lies at an altitude of about 5,413ft (1,650m) amidst untouched nature with breathtaking views of the Zugspitze massif, as well as the Vorderer Tajakopf, Vorderer Drachenkopf, and Ehrwalder Sonnenspitze. The easiest way to reach the lake is from the neighboring municipalities of Lermoos or Ehrwald: from the parking lot on the southern outskirts, a 5 mile

Mrs T: "Enjoying the Zugspitze view together from a relaxation lounge at the Mohr escape—I'm loving it!"

(8.5km) forest track traverses the Ehrwalder Alm, ascending about 1,968ft (600m) in altitude. Shortly before reaching the Seebensee, you will pass the Seebenalm, which operates in the summer season, so a hearty snack is a possible reward on the way back.

Tyrolean Zugspitze Cable Car
(approx. 4½ miles/7km)

Although at 9,718ft (2,962m) the Zugspitze is Germany's highest mountain, the Tyrolean Zugspitze cable car also takes you up from the Austrian side, and has done so for a bit longer than from Bavaria, namely since July 1926. The first cable car in the Tyrol, it only went up to 9,203ft (2,805m), whereas the new construction, finished in July 1991, goes all the way up to the western summit. In the local mountain station, a small museum explains the technically complex construction of the two cable cars. The present, longer route also opens up the glacier ski resort on Zugspitzplatt beyond the western summit for guests in Lermoos or Ehrwald.

Reutte
(approx. 12½ miles/20km)

The largest town near Lermoos is the market town of Reutte, located about 12½ miles (20km) to the northwest. All around the main market square, the Obermarkt, there are a number of interesting houses, such as the district authority's headquarters with its late 18th-century curved gable and the three-story Gasthof Schwarzer Adler with its neo-classical painted façade. A highlight of a very special kind extends on the southern outskirts of Reutte: Highline179. Some 1,322ft (403m) long and up to 377ft (115m) high, this is the world's longest pedestrian suspension bridge, linking the ruins of Ehrenberg Castle, built in 1296, and the 17th-century Fort Claudia, which once protected the transit route through the Alps used since Roman times.

Tiroler Zugspitz Golf
(approx. 1¼ miles/2km)

About 1.2 miles (2 km) to the east is the Tiroler Zugspitz Golf Course. Gently embedded in the landscape, this 9-hole course, on which 18-hole laps are also possible, offers ideal conditions for beginners and advanced golfers alike. All around there are fantastic views of the Zugspitze massif to be enjoyed. The modern course has a well-balanced mix of par-3, par-4, and par-5 holes through a generous driving range. If you want to play on several days, it's best to buy the Wetterstein4Golf Greenfee Card, which includes three other courses in the region. And if, in time-honored tradition, you intend to play

↑ You can save yourself the first (and not so spectacular in terms of scenery) 1,312ft (400m) of steep uphill walking from Ehrwald to Sebensee with a ticket for the Ehrwalder Almbahn. And if you want to continue past the lake, you can take your Brotzeit snack at the Coburger Hütte after another fairly steep 820ft (250m) in altitude.

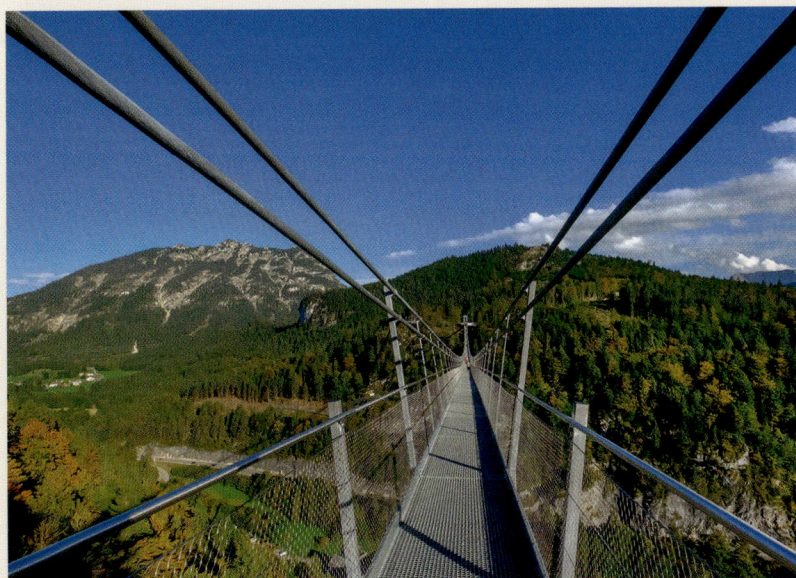

↑ The path from Fort Claudia to the ruins of Ehrenberg Castle over the pedestrian suspension bridge Highline179 near Reutte is spectacular. Allow about 10 to 15 minutes to cross the bridge, including stops for enjoying the views, over a distance of 1,312ft (400m) at some 328ft (100m) above the abyss— not a path for those who are afraid of heights.

the "19th hole" at the end of the game, there's the attractive Golfino restaurant in the clubhouse, with modern architecture that is reminiscent of a golf ball!

HOTEL KITZHOF
Kitzbühel, Austria

The Kitzhof Mountain Design Resort—a large complex with the feel of a boutique hotel—is situated on the edge of Kitzbühel and is a major destination for skiers in the winter and mountain walkers in the summer.

hotel info:

Hotel Kitzhof Mountain
Design Resort
Schwarzseestr. 8-10
A-6370 Kitzbühel
Tel.: +43 5356 632110
Mail: info@hotel-kitzhof.com
Web: www.hotel-kitzhof.com

charging facilities:

2 Tesla DeC (Tesla only)
1 Tesla DeC (all EVs)

The valley is vast, and the view on both sides of the road as you drive to Hotel Kitzhof sweeps over the spectacular Tyrolean alpine scenery—a landscape that is just as expansive as the hotel itself. Its 168 rooms are spread over several buildings, giving the complex a charming Tyrolean-village style. The relaxed ambience is underlined by the warmth and friendliness of the entire hotel team. The tastefully appointed rooms leave nothing to be desired—depending on category, there is everything from a professional coffee machine and a comfortable sitting area to a free-standing bathtub with a second television in the bathroom, and much more. The

Mrs T: "*There are magazines and books for those who like to read—so you could just check yourself into the Kitzhof for a few weeks and get very cozy.*"

Weisser Hirsch, the hotel's outstanding restaurant, serves breakfast and dinner. The range of fresh dishes on offer is extensive, and the view from the tables of the garden and mountains is simply magical. Also of note is the fact that the modern spa facility, with large indoor pool and saunas, is open until 10 p.m., so you can work on your fitness even after dinner—unless of course you're relaxing by the open fire in the hotel bar.

AROUND KITZBÜHEL
Austria

The perfect holiday region in Tyrol

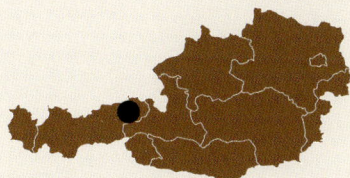

Kitzbühel is a fashionable destination for winter sports, and you may well see some famous faces descending the mountain. The resort town and surrounding countryside are simply beautiful, and not only for their great winter sports facilities. In summer, you can hike, go mountaineering, or swing a golf club.

Hahnenkamm
(approx. ½ mile/1km)

The valley station in the legendary Hahnenkamm ski region is just a ten-minute walk from the hotel. You'll find the starting point for the extremely steep Streif slope at the mountain station, where the world's best skiers vie for victory in the annual Hahnenkamm alpine ski race in January. "Average" skiers are meanwhile advised to try and descend the Streif family slope, the Kampen that branches off it, or the Asten, with all four slopes ending in a 492ft (150m) wide area down at the valley station. The Hahnenkamm is also a popular place for Kitzbühel visitors in summer, and boasts several scenic hiking trails offering spectacular views and numerous cozy lodges where you can drop in for a hearty meal.

Golfclub Kitzbühel
(approx. 1¼ miles/2km)

Founded in 1955, the Kitzbühel Golf Club is the most traditional of the three golf clubs in the area and open to all levels. The nine-hole course, which features mature trees and lots of water features, is located at the base of Schloss Kaps (Kaps Castle), and has hosted a number of championships over the years. Play a round here and you'll be surrounded by stunning mountain backdrops—including the Jochberg Mountains, the Wilder Kaiser,

Mr T: "Kitzbühel is a beautiful village with some very chic boutiques, lots of hiking trails, and world-renowned ski slopes."

and the Hahnenkamm—at almost every turn, with great views of the town below. The terrace at the adjacent Steakhouse Kaps, situated between the tee box and the ninth green, is the perfect place to end an enjoyable day of golfing over a cold drink and a delicious international meal.

to drink

The short journey to the British capital takes just five minutes: once you've entered the house, typically Tyrolean on the outside, and you see the street sign Oxford St. W1 inside above the typical pub bar, you've arrived. Founded by an Englishman and his Kitzbühel wife in 1976, locals and tourists meet at The Londoner for a traditional beer, an aromatic gin, or a whiskey throughout the year. Unlike London, the curfew here is at 4 a.m.!

The Londoner
Franz-Reisch-Str. 4
www.thelondoner.at

HOTEL POST BEZAU BY SUSANNE KAUFMANN

Bezau in the Bregenz Forest, Austria

The Hotel Post Bezau by Susanne Kaufmann is located in the middle of the picturesque Bregenz Forest. Thanks to its combination of purist design and sustainability, as well as wellness, health, and beauty treatments, you will immediately feel at home.

hotel info:

Hotel Post Bezau by
Susanne Kaufmann
Brugg 35
A-6870 Bezau
Tel.: +43 5514 2207-0
Mail: welcome@
hotelpostbezau.com
Web: www.
hotelpostbezau.com

charging facilities:

2 Tesla DeC (Tesla only)
2 Tesla DeC (all EVs)

Hotel Post Bezau was first established about 150 years ago, but it was only in the summer of 2019 that it reopened with its new branding as Hotel Post Bezau by Susanne Kaufmann. The revised name is a reference to the new approach, which involves more intensively integrating the holistic wellness and beauty concept devised by the hotel's owner and name-giver, who is also known for her line of organic body and skin products. The property, which comprises a historic Bregenz Forest house and a modern, wood-clad extension, is an ideal place to unplug and unwind in the seclusion of the mountains. Featuring an abundance of wood and large panoramic

Mrs T: "You enter an entirely different universe in the all-white, modern beauty area. All the treatments on offer are of the highest quality."

windows, the room designs are as conducive to this new concept as the highly-qualified hotel team's commitment. Place your trust in the soothing hands of the experts at the on-site spa, where all treatments use locally sourced products—much like the restaurant in the main building. Whether starters, mains (including vegetarian options), or desserts, great emphasis is placed on ensuring ingredients are natural and sustainable.

AROUND BEZAU
Austria

The peace of the forest and the happiness of the mountains

Bregenz Forest offers ski resorts, the best hiking trails, cycling routes for every level, and all the recreational opportunities you'd expect of an Alpine region. It's quieter and more relaxed than its neighbors—while offering great food, as the number of excellent restaurants proves.

Bregenz (approx. 21 miles/34km)

Bregenz lies about a half hour's drive from the hotel, on the eastern shores of Lake Constance, between the local Pfänder mountain and the Swiss border (see page 205). The capital of the Vorarlberg region is more significant than you may perhaps expect from a city with a population of barely 30,000. The Bregenzer Festspiele performing arts festival, with productions on impressive floating stages, and the Bregenzer Frühling, a large dance festival featuring participants from all over the world, are both internationally acclaimed. And as you stroll through the inner city, we recommend taking a short detour to the promenade and harbor at Lake Constance, or, alternatively, paying a visit to the award-winning Kunsthaus Bregenz contemporary art gallery.

Bregenz Forest (approx. 3 miles/5km)

Bezau is part of the Bregenz Forest, a rolling landscape (today characterized more by grassland and scattered townships) in the catchment area of the Bregenzer Ach River at the northern edge of the Alps. This makes the Bregenz Forest a popular hiking district and mountain-biking destination during the summer months, while thrilling skiing enthusiasts during the winter. But for all its popularity, the atmosphere here remains calmer and qui-

Mr T: "The wellness area has a pool on the ground floor, saunas and a whirlpool above, and an outdoor saltwater pool at the top."

eter than in Tyrol or at the Arlberg. And as the Bregenz Forest is traditionally dairy country, the *Käsestrasse Bregenzerwald* (Bregenz Forest Cheese Route) brings together farmers and restaurateurs selling the famed mountain cheese so highly regarded by gourmets.

to eat

Gourmet chef, Gabi Strahammer serves excellent food at the well known Schulhus (which means schoolhouse) restaurant in Krumbach, a former school, less than 30 minutes' drive from Bezau. Using regional produce, she creates delicious meals, without the need for fancy or exotic surprises. The meals are accompanied by wines from the well-stocked cellar, run by her husband, Herbert. Not surprisingly many wines are from Austrian vineyards.

Schulhus
Glatzegg 58,
A-6942 Krumbach
www.schulhus.at

↑ The Winterstaude at 6,158ft (1,877m) altitude is the highest point of the ridge which rises north of Bezau. A beautiful but challenging hike runs along the ridge from one peak to another.

Wälderbähnle Museum Train
(approx. ½ mile/1km)

More than 100 years ago, the railroad from Bregenz to Bezau was the only major transport link in the Bregenz Forest. These days, a historic steam train featuring a few carriages of the Wälderbähnle—as the museum train is affectionately known—operates along the 3 mile (5km) stretch of old track from Bezau to Schwarzenberg and back every weekend from late May to early October. Additional services run on Wednesdays in July and August, and on special occasions, such as December 6, when St. Nicholas and his companion Knecht Ruprecht distribute small gifts on the train. The Wälderbähnle can also be booked for weddings, birthdays, and other occasions.

Baumgarten and Alpe Niedere
(approx. 1.2 miles/2km)

Bezau's local mountain is the 5,410ft (1,649m) high Baumgarten, on which the Bezau cable car operates (see page 203). Once at the top, you can either head straight to the panoramic restaurant and enjoy the view of the surrounding peaks and down into the valley—or you can "earn" your snack by first taking a small circular hike. Follow a well-marked path to the Hintere Niedere, and then farther left to the Vordere Niedere and the Fallkopf lookout, before reaching the small mountain chapel and the Alpe Niedere. On days when conditions are suitable, paragliders start their flights from here. Those who prefer walking, on the other hand, will find themselves back at the Baumgarten mountain station within minutes. By now, it's definitely time for a bite to eat!

Bezau Local History Museum
(approx. ½ mile/1km)

The Bezau Local History Museum is located on the southern outskirts of Bezau, and is housed in an 18th-century shingled farmhouse typical of the Bregenz Forest region. Stepping into the kitchen and living areas of the museum is like taking a journey back through time, and gives you a good idea of the everyday lives of rural farming folk of that period. Local people cooked over an open fire, and made their tasty cheese on the *Senngelegenheit* cheese-making facility using the alpine cows' milk. The lounge and dining room was heated by a traditional clay wood stove, and the wood-paneled master bedroom had a wooden four-poster bed. Historic costumes and traditional embroidery from the Bregenz Forest, coupled with agricultural equipment, round off this unique snapshot of times past.

BERGLAND DESIGN- & WELLNESSHOTEL

Sölden, Austria

The Bergland Design- and Wellnesshotel Sölden is located in the Tyrolean holiday resort of Sölden. This family-run property is ideal for relaxing in the spa or for pursuing activities in the mountains, which surround the hotel.

hotel info:

Bergland Design- and
Wellnesshotel Sölden
Dorfstr. 114
A-6450 Sölden
Tel.: +43 5254 2240-0
Mail: info@
bergland-soelden.at
Web: www.
bergland-soelden.at

charging facilities:

2 Tesla DeC (Tesla only)
1 Tesla DeC (all EVs)

In the heart of the Ötztal Alps, the Bergland Design- and Wellnesshotel in Sölden boasts five-star comfort that impressed even the likes of James Bond actor Daniel Craig when he was shooting *Spectre* here. Run by Elisabeth and Sigi Grüner and their family, the modern property's rooms and suites skillfully incorporate elements of the local alpine environment into their design. Wood, wool, and warm, natural colors make for a highly unique and harmonious feeling of wellbeing and ease, while the Sky Spa, the hotel's 18,300 sq ft (1,700sq m) rooftop wellness facility, offers pure relaxation with its panoramic views of the surrounding mountains. Whether it be the pool, sauna, yoga, fitness, beauty treatments, or massages,

Mrs T: "Start the day in the large pool with panoramic alpine views and in the evening relax in the sauna with views of the Tyrolean mountains—fab!"

this hotel has something for everyone. And those who enjoy outdoor sporting activities can start hiking or biking straight from the hotel's doorstep or, in winter, head out to the ski slopes. After working up an appetite, a tasty multi-course menu awaits guests in the evening. The Black Sheep gourmet restaurant, with its tasting menu crafted by head chef Stephan Muhr, and Wine & Dine, with its à-la-carte offering, are also open during the winter months.

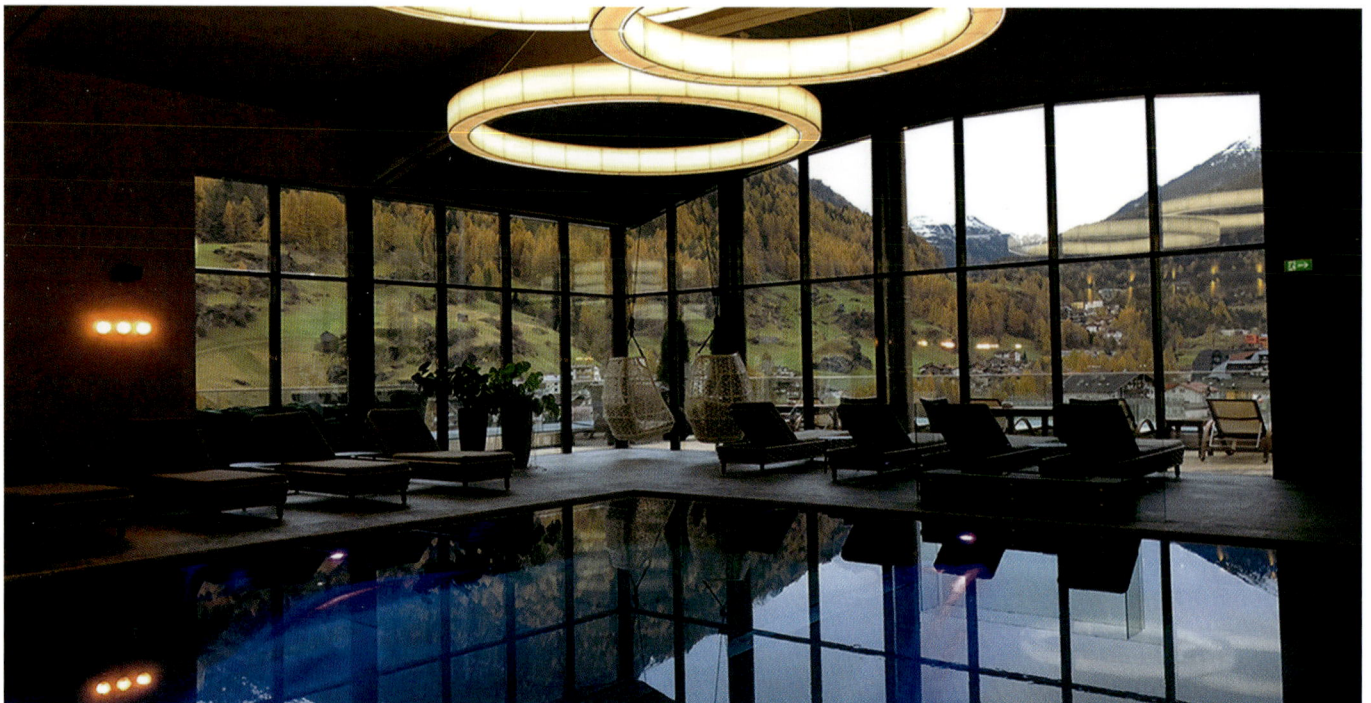

AROUND SÖLDEN
Austria

In the high alpine border region between Austria and Italy

There are many passes over the Alps. Most visitors use the tunneled stretch under the St. Gotthard or the Brenner Pass, which is 8,117ft (1,370m) high. Much more exciting, however, is a drive over the Timmelsjoch. Here, the main point is not arriving, but the journey itself.

007 Elements (approx. 3 miles/5km)

"The name's Bond, James Bond." These iconic words have been frequently repeated on the Gaislachkogl since the summer of 2018. Situated at 9,974ft (3,040m) above sea level, 007 Elements unlocks a world dedicated to the British undercover agent, the futuristic and largely underground complex reminiscent of a Bond villain's secret headquarters. Nine rooms over two levels, featuring video installations, original equipment, a re-enacted action scene involving a plane (below right), sound effects, and interactive stations relating to the 2015 Bond film *Spectre*, which was filmed partly on the Gaislachkogl, along with more than twenty other films from the Bond series, are sure to get every Bond fan's heart racing. Regain your composure by taking in the silent vastness of the Ötztal Alps.

Timmelsjoch High Alpine Road (approx. 9¼ miles/15km, Obergurgl to Merano approx. 37 miles/60km)

South of Sölden, it's not far to the Italian border. The Timmelsjoch high mountain pass starts at Untergurgl, heading up some 8,200ft (2,500m). The panoramic tollway is considered one of the most beautiful in all of Tyrol. So it's all the more fitting to be able to drive through this magical landscape quietly and emission-free, using electric power to navi-

Mr T: "Up there, high in the mountains, we were—so to speak—in bed with Her Majesty's secret agent."

gate the twelve hairpin bends on the Austrian side up to the top—passing a pedestrian bridge jutting far out over the Ötztal Valley, and an art installation serving as a reminder of the many smugglers who once operated here. At the top, the Pass Museum provides information on the road's construction.

to eat
The perfect complement to a visit of 007 Elements is a stop at the Ice Q on the Gaislachkogl. The highest-lying award-winning restaurant in Austria, which served as the backdrop for the Bond film *Spectre*, offers gourmet cuisine.

Ice Q
Gaislachkoglbahn
Mountain Station
Dorfstraße 115
A-6450 Sölden
www.iceq.at

↑ The Wildspitze, at 12,382ft (3,774m) the highest elevation, overlooks the Ötztal Alps and the Ötztal Nature Park. The second highest mountain in Austria, it is climbed in summer and winter—the latter is a challenging undertaking that takes you over glaciers and difficult terrain.

to celebrate

Since the 2000/2001 season, the Sölden races for the Alpine Ski World Cup on the Rettenbachferner have kicked off the event each year. The men's and women's giant slalom races reach from the starting point at over 9,843ft (3,000m) to the finish at 8,793ft (2,680m) altitude. Spectators arrive by shuttle bus to the finish arena, where they welcome the skiers.

Alpine Ski World Cup Giant Slalom season opener, Sölden
www.soelden.com/skiweltcup
End of October

The Fernrohr ("Telescope") and Granat ("Garnet") installations are situated on the Italian side, and provide stunning panoramic views.

Ötzi Village in Umhausen (approx. 15½ miles/25km)

The 5,250-year-old mummy known as Ötzi was found in a glacier on the Tilsenjoch in 1991. Today, Ötzi Village, an open-air archaeological park in Umhausen, showcases life in the Neolithic period. From May to October, reconstructions and models bring prehistoric everyday routines to life, while staff members demonstrate bread-baking, fire-making, and archery skills. There are also various multi-day courses where participants can make their own objects, such as baskets or flint knives.

AREA 47 (approx. 23½ miles/38km)

AREA 47, at the point where the Ötztaler Ache River opens out into the Inn River, is the largest open-air recreation park in Austria, and the perfect place for adrenalin junkies. The park has five sections—Outdoor, Climbing, Freeride, Water, and Wake. In the Outdoor area you can raft down the Ötztaler Ache in a rubber dinghy, while the Climbing section allows you to conquer the country's highest 89ft (27m) high-ropes course or the equally lofty climbing tower. Freeride involves taking mountain bikes or E-MTBs along various single tracks in the Ötztal Valley. Water, meanwhile, offers some comparatively sedate attractions, such as a 56ft (17m) high water ramp or water slides. Rounding things off is Wake, where a circuit of more than 1,312ft (400m) introduces wakeboarding, a mix of waterskiing and surfing. In keeping with the outdoor vibe, a BBQ restaurant takes care of adventurers' culinary needs.

Ötztal Nature Park (approx. 9¼ miles/15km)

The Ötztal Nature Park encompasses all the nature reserves located in the southward ascending valley, stretching as far up as the 12,382 ft (3,774m) high Ötztaler Wildspitze. The villages of Vent and Obergurgl—the latter also being Austria's highest Kirchdorf ("church village")—both provide excellent starting points for easy as well as more challenging hikes through this part of the Tyrolean mountains. The modern natural history exhibition in the newly opened Naturpark Haus in Längenfeld, meanwhile, is an ideal source of information before or after a day on the trail. The facility covering an area of 32,230sq ft (300sq m) is specifically focused on the flora, fauna, and geology of the Ötztal Valley.

TRAVELING BY ELECTRIC CAR

An orientation guide for newcomers, those making the switch, and those who already have some e-xperience

In today's age of global climate change, exploring the world emission-free and more consciously is an excellent way of traveling more sustainably in a double sense. Europe is the perfect starting point for such a journey. Where else can you find so many different cultures and such a wide range of tourist attractions?

So here's our first tip: Don't wait—get going and start driving!

During our own tour, we gained a number of relevant insights that will be of particular interest to newcomers with electric cars—meaning your travels can be sustainable and full of battery-powered energy, allowing you to reach your destination feeling calm and relaxed.

Electric cars— what you need to know

Electromobility is still a highly controversial topic in all the countries we visited on our tour. Unfortunately, even the press and many supposed experts keep arguing against electric cars and their future. It is evident this has unsettled a number of people, so we want to start by clarifying a few general questions.

What exactly is an "EV"?

In common speech, "EV" is often used synonymously with electric cars. **"EV"** is short for "electric vehicle," and thus denotes all types of vehicles that are powered by one or more electric engines. Hybrid vehicles, on the other hand, are not members of the family of electric vehicles, *per se*, as a second, non-electric engine is combined with an electric one in these vehicles—hence the term, "hybrid."

Interestingly, vehicles powered purely by electricity actually existed long before Tesla began revolutionizing the automotive market. After the steam engine, the electric engine started being used in vehicles as early as the first few decades of the 19th century, and thus well before the combustion engine. The fact that electric cars failed to establish themselves then, despite their various advantages, was primarily due to the fact that battery technology at the time was still inadequate.

What advantages do electric cars offer me as a user?

Apart from several other positive attributes, electric cars offer a wide range of benefits to their owners in daily use. Firstly, it is cheaper to run an electric car than its combustion-engine counterpart. Electricity prices right across Europe are already much lower than those for gasoline or diesel. Depending on the country you live in, you can also make further savings in insurance premiums and benefit from tax concessions.

Electric cars do not possess any complex combustion engine, exhaust system, starter, spark plug, clutch, gearbox, or anything comparable, meaning a drastic reduction in the likelihood of needing repairs. Regenerative braking puts very little strain on the brakes, and oil changes are dispensed with entirely. This results in much lower overall maintenance costs and minimal periods of time when your car is stuck at the garage. Companies like Tesla, who can perform diagnostics remotely, and who also offer a mobile repair service, save their customers the further hassle of having to get the car to and from a garage.

When driving, you can actually perceive the difference with your own senses. The noise level is considerably lower, and you feel a lot less vibration compared to an internal combustion engine vehicle. Electric cars also create less of a noticeable smell, as they do not produce any exhaust fumes while driving and you also don't have to worry about toxic fumes from oil, gas, or diesel. And once you really step "on the gas", the smile on your face will be proof enough that driving an electric car is also a lot more fun in terms of vehicle dynamics. Safety is another important criterion, and Tesla cars are considered among the safest in the world.

Are electric cars really more environmentally friendly than gas and diesel vehicles?

In our view, the answer to this highly disputed question is once again a loud and clear affirmative: "YES!"

But we believe it is important to back up our personal opinion with information from a recognized institution. Let's take a look at Germany—after all, the country is Europe's automotive powerhouse bar none. Based on turnover, Germany's automotive industry is today by far the country's most important, and even though local car manufacturers may have been a little late in waking up to the electric future, electric cars will end up playing a key role in that country.

The fundamental question of whether electric cars are environmentally friendly has, of course, also been raised in Germany, and the German Federal Ministry for the Environment, Nature Conservation, and

Mr & Mrs T: "It is our mission to explore the world in a Tesla, inspire others, and promote a more sustainable lifestyle."

Nuclear Safety (BMU) has already provided a good answer. On its website, the BMU recently published some informational videos (see the links on our website) explaining the matter in plain, simple language. This BMU information is consistent with our own current understanding of the facts and the situation as it stands right now.

↑ Mr & Mrs T on the road in a fully-electric Tesla Model S

E-mobility is utterly essential if we want to achieve climate change targets. Electric cars use considerably less energy than other mobility solutions, and thus constitute a smart alternative. Not only is this significantly more climate-friendly overall, but it also saves money. These statements are already valid today, and they will grow all the more important as sustainable energy becomes increasingly prevalent in the future.

Although there is still considerable room for improvement in terms of the air pollutants generated during manufacturing, it can already be said today that "a modern-day e-car generates about 25 percent less emissions than a gas-powered car throughout its lifetime from production to final disposal," and, "in 2025, new electric cars are expected to produce 40 percent less carbon emissions than gas-powered cars and one-third less than diesel vehicles." So, the advantages will be even greater because the cleaner the electricity, the cleaner the electric car.

The car must, of course, also be capable of storing the electricity, which brings us to the topic of batteries and the raw materials necessary for producing them. There is often talk of raw materials not being available in large enough quantities, particularly because lithium and cobalt are too rare to be able to produce batteries in sufficient numbers. The BMU's response to this, however, is that "there is enough, even if demand increases." What is critical, then, is how we mine these raw materials. "We sometimes tend to forget that mobility, as we currently know it, does not always have the most ecologically or socially sound basis."

↑ Tesla Superchargers facilitate high-speed energy top-ups while on the road

This is a fundamental problem, which also concerns the production of oil. Electric cars, however, have one key advantage: We are still only in the early days of developing and manufacturing suitable energy storages, whereas very little can be done to make combustion engines more efficient. "Sometimes it will even be possible to fully substitute critical raw materials by other materials. And, of course, switching to electric cars will also mean using much fewer fossil fuels, such as petroleum." At the end of an electric car's life, many of the raw materials, particularly those used for the batteries, can also be recycled and re-introduced to the cycle. "And there needs to be a fair comparison! Using electricity instead of oil is a major gain in itself!"

An overview of the charging infrastructure in Europe

Most of the questions we were asked during our tour were related to charging. We want to answer the four most frequent ones, from a traveler's perspective.

Where can I charge my car?

Electric cars can generally be charged wherever there is a suitable electric socket. As even a conventional household socket will suffice, you can theoretically charge you car virtually anywhere.

Because you are usually more focused on your journey and your destination when you're traveling, you'll most likely be recharging at fast-charging stations, especially during longer trips. And provided you have chosen hotels that are well equipped and prepared for guests arriving by electric car, your own car will be recharging overnight while you enjoy

Side note: The Tesla charging network

Tesla has one of the world's fastest and largest networks of chargers, consisting of Superchargers and Destination Chargers. Superchargers are Tesla fast-charging stations, usually located along major travel routes, to support long distance travel. Destination Chargers act as a power source once you have arrived at your destination. These are typically found in places where people are likely to spend more time, such as hotels, restaurants, or shopping malls.

While the Superchargers can currently only be used by Tesla vehicles, many Destination Charging partners across Europe have installed wall boxes where other electric cars can also be charged.

Another practical aspect is the fact that all Tesla charging locations are shown on the car's onboard navigation map (including real-time Supercharger availability) as well as on the map on Tesla's website. Once you have connected your car for charging, you can use the Tesla app to monitor and control the charging process from anywhere. You are automatically notified when charging is complete.

Thanks to the extremely well-developed Tesla charging infrastructure, we were able to complete our tour accross Europe without the need to use any third-party provider. Anyone who, unlike us, didn't include Supercharger use as part of their purchase package can still enjoy travel at a much lower cost, without having to worry about any tedious payment processes. The Supercharger will recognize your car, and you will simply be billed through your Tesla customer account.

a nice meal and recover from a day's sightseeing.

Is the charging infrastructure adequate?

At the present time, the answer to this question still depends to some degree on which type of electric car you are driving, although soon that will not make much of a difference anymore. Even considerable distances no longer present a major problem, especially in well-developed tourist areas.

↑ Tesla Destination Chargers allow you to charge your car once you have arrived at your destination

Aside from Tesla, other car manufacturers and energy companies have now also realized how important it is to provide a reliable, well-developed charging infrastructure. In addition to the large-scale expansion of the network of fast-charging stations, they are now also striving to simplify the overall billing process with regard to existing charging points. Some manufacturers, for instance, enable you to charge your vehicle, and pay for this, at many different stations across Europe using just one single charging card. This dispenses with the need to register with a multitude of different providers, and it also means that you will only receive one consolidated bill at the end.

On our own travels through Europe, we were able to observe that the charging infrastructure was being expanded everywhere and in all the countries we visited. New, faster charging stations are being added to the network by the day, and so it is only a matter of time before finding easily accessible charging stations at every street corner will be as normal as gas stations are today.

But for those who still have their doubts about the future of electric cars in terms of charging infrastructure, it is useful to take a quick look back at automotive history for an objective perspective.

Let's step back to the year 1886, the year the first "horseless wagon" was patented by Carl Benz. Who would have imagined back then what we would find on our streets today? When Bertha Benz took her husband's vehicle out for its first long-distance drive just two years after the patenting, there was still not a single gas station around.

In other words, it certainly won't be an inadequate charging infrastructure that dashes the success of electric cars since this is already being established and/or expanded everywhere on a vast scale. As such, just as it was wrong in 1886 to think the automobile, in that form, would never catch on, so it would be equally misguided today to assume that electric cars are not the vehicles of the future. That would make you just as mistaken as Germany's last emperor, Kaiser Wilhelm II, when he said "I believe in the horse. The automobile is no more than a transitory phenomenon."

How long does it take to charge an electric car?

The question of how long it takes to charge an electric car is usually raised in relation to a full charging process; that is, when the battery needs to be charged from 0 percent to 100 percent. But it is actually not really possible to make a direct comparison with the refueling of an internal combustion engine car in terms of the overall time it takes, for electric cars are often charged by the way, when time is not a factor.

One of our friends once described it as follows: "It takes about ten seconds to charge an electric car: five seconds to connect the car to the charging station, and another five seconds to unplug it when charging is completed!" Mostly, the time in between can be utilized efficiently. Unlike at a gas station, you don't have to wait at the charging point during the charging process; you can attend to more pressing—or interesting—matters.

During our tour, we would generally top up at Tesla Superchargers after about two or three hours of driving, for about ten to

Side note: How to charge correctly

- **Recharge on time:** Don't wait until the battery is completely empty, or until you need to charge it to 100 percent in order to reach your destination. Interim charges will save you time and also protect the battery.
- **Charge opportunistically**: Whenever possible, charge at a time when you are taking a break anyway or when you have an errand to complete. You do what you want or need to do; the car doesn't dictate your life.
- **Only charge as much as necessary:** At fast-charging stations, you only need to charge enough to reach your next charging point, with just a little in reserve—unless you yourself need more time at the location to do other things.
- **Always factor in a little reserve when charging**: Even if the car is showing that you have enough energy to reach your next destination, it is better to charge for a few extra miles. You may find yourself in traffic jams, having to take detours, or using more than you thought. You will also feel more relaxed knowing there is still enough power left in the battery.
- **Charge little and fast on the go, but often and slowly overnight:** Fast chargers are particularly practical if a single initial charge is not enough to get you to your destination. Otherwise, we recommend charging the car overnight at home, or, when traveling, at your hotel. This will not only save you time by charging "while you sleep," but it will also save you money (charging is free at many hotels). Charging slower is also gentler on the battery.

twenty minutes at a time. And we made most of these stops tied in with us taking a break that we needed anyway.

Charging time generally hinges on four main factors:
- the capacity of the battery that is fitted in your car
- your vehicle's charging technology
- the maximum output of the charging station you are at
- your car's current charging phase.

Under otherwise equal conditions, larger batteries will take longer than smaller ones to charge fully. But, of course, large batteries also provide longer ranges, allowing you to drive farther on your journeys, without the need to top up quite as often.

The car's built-in charging technology determines the speed at which the vehicle, or rather its battery, can absorb energy from the charging point. The charging station's performance, on the other hand, determines the maximum possible energy inflow. The "weaker link" of the two systems thus dictates the maximum charging speed under otherwise identical conditions on each occasion.

The fourth aspect that you should bear in mind is the fact that the charging speed slows down considerably as soon as a charging level of 80 percent is reached. It is worth remembering, however, that the battery very rarely needs to be charged to a full 100 percent. This is generally only done when absolutely necessary to reach your next destination or charging location.

What do I need in order to charge my car?

Every electric car is delivered including all the associated basic equipment like charging cable and adapter. Whether you will need additional charging cables and/or adapters depends on the vehicle you have chosen and the charging stations you wish to use on a regular basis. Drivers of non-Tesla vehicles have also confirmed to us that you will quickly work out what works best for your particular needs. As such, it can be a good idea to borrow the accessories you think you need from friends, and wait with a purchase until you know if they are truly required.

When traveling around Europe, however, you can expect most fast-charging stations to now be equipped with a type-2 and/or "Combined Charging System" (CCS) connector as a standard. Since the relevant

Mr & Mrs T: "Acting more sustainably should not stop with driving an electric car, but it is a good start!"

cables and plugs are typically also integrated into fast-charging stations, therefore you won't have to carry your own cable around with you in order to charge. It is possible, however, that you need to have an adapter for your vehicle. Most new electric cars that are now sold in Europe have either a type-2 or CSS connection.

Our tip: Don't buy any charging accessories until you know what you will actually need.

Properly planning your EV journey

Based on our own experience, we can wholeheartedly say that traveling by electric car is both much more fun and more relaxing! In other words, your vacation starts immediately once you get into your car and start driving, instead of after arriving at your holiday destination follwing a stressed out journey. And it doesn't always have to be a two week e-road-trip; even a weekend getaway will fully convince you.

What should you think of prior to a longer journey in an electric car?

In addition to everything you would think about before any kind of road trip, it is particularly important to remember that the better you plan your journey, the more relaxed you and your passengers will feel when arriving at your destination.

Make sure to choose the best possible route before setting off. Factor in sufficient breaks, and don't forget to take into account potential stops along the way, because making a detour to an interesting attraction is often well worth it. After all, being able to change your route and seeing additional sights is one of the main advantages of an independent road trip.

Once you have made your plan, you can tie it back with your vehicle's framework conditions and then decide where and for how long you will stop for charging (if needed at all). You will find that you end up needing a break more often than your car needs recharging. This is particularly true if you are driving an electric car with a very long range, like we do.

↑ The 3-pillar model of sustainability

What tools may be useful when planning your route?

Depending on the manufacturer and vehicle type, routes can be planned directly in the car, or via a corresponding app, respectively, on the manufacturer's website. In addition, there are a great number of external providers who also offer route-planning solutions, some of which even enable you to tailor your route plans to your vehicle model, battery performance, and personal preferences. For your convenience, we have put together a small selection of relevant links on our website.

Our tip: Prior to purchasing an electric car, we highly recommend checking whether the manufacturer's solution suits your personal needs, and how well it is adjusted to the available charging network.

Sustainability

Only very few words are used, overused, and sometimes even abused more often and in more contexts than "sustainability." Acting more sustainably should be of interest to us all, as it is fundamental to everyone's survival! It should also be so much more than just a marketing effort; many companies, in particular, like to undertake when striving for a positive external perception.

What we learned about sustainability being on the road

One of our main reasons to travel the world in an electric car was to learn more about the subject of sustainability as a whole. Tesla's mission to accelerate the world's transition to sustainable energy also played a very important role in our decision, and gave us pause for thought right from the beginning.

More than ever, it has become crucial to act sustainably as a global society. In many countries, we are living well beyond our means—at an ecological, economical, and social level. If we want humankind to survive, and to keep the system going over the long term, all three aspects (see the "Three-pillar model" of sustainability on the page 217) will need to be taken into account. If we neglect one or more of these "pillars," the entire system becomes unbalanced.

But what does that actually mean for each of us as individuals? With that question in mind we set off to our tour around Europe, trying to find answers along the way.

The most important finding turned out to be one so obvious that we all unfortunately tend to overlook or ignore it. Far too often, we think we only have little capacity to change things ourselves—but that is simply not true! We can all change the world every single day, and each person making their own small contribution within their sphere of influence is better than doing nothing at all. Don't expect yourself or others to be able to, or even to have to, act 100 percent perfectly each and every time. Numerous small actions always end up having a greater effect than one big action that never comes about. So it's best to start with ourselves!

We believe that living more sustainably can and should ideally be a huge amount of fun, because if that's the case, you will automatically want to behave in an even more sustainable manner. We, too, used to have a completely different idea of such a change in behavior, because it smacked of a wagging finger admonishing us instead of the better option that would have made it so easy for us. This became clear to us on our very first Tesla test drive. This was a company

launching a product that was more sustainable than any other comparable vehicle option—and because it was also designed to be a lot of fun to drive, we immediately went for it.

In our case, purchasing a fully electric car thus opened the door to a more sustainable lifestyle. We've been traveling differently ever since—both on the road and in life in general. We're still not perfect—and probably never will be—but we're much more aware and definitely live more sustainably than we did before.

During our trip it became clear that many hotels we visited are making concerted efforts to not only visibly embody sustainability by using towels more than once, but also to act more sustainably in the background whenever possible. It is the guest, however, who carries the most influence here, so never underestimate your own power.

Although it is impossible to address this issue in detail here (that would probably need a book in itself), it was still important for us to mention it. Why? Because even when traveling, it can still be very easy to act more sustainably if you start looking for better options and consciously choosing these.

How can I make my own traveling more sustainable?

Using an electric car in itself is already much more environmentally friendly. Therefore it is having a direct positive impact on the **ecological** side of your road trip. Those who want to do even more, however, can, for instance, offset their remaining carbon footprint by working with our partner myclimate, who ensured our entire tour was carbon-neutral.

By doing so, you actively support consultancy, education, and climate-protection projects all over the world.

In terms of vehicle costs per mile, electric cars once again usually tend to outclass their non-electric counterparts, particularly given that the **economic** effect becomes even more apparent the more you travel. The money you save can then be put to other use, instead of literally going up in smoke by using an internal combustion engine car.

But what is the **social** aspect of sustainability all about? It's primarily about people, because, after all, the reason you're taking a road trip is to recharge your own batteries, and that ideally starts on the journey itself—at least if you follow our philosophy.

Our tip: Make the journey the destination by traveling more consciously instead of simply getting from A to B as quickly as possible. It is relaxing to drive an electric car, and we ourselves have never before arrived at our destinations feeling so calm and utterly stress-free. You cruise through the beautiful scenery silently, appreciating what you see, without any gear-changing, and, thanks to seamless acceleration, extra smoothly. It is an ultra-pleasant driving experience, and every stop along the way is a great opportunity to discover something new.

Choose an attractive route, not the supposedly fastest, because the most beautiful road conjures up a smile on your face while driving. Explore attractions as you go, and plan stages that are comfortable for you and your body. Take regular breaks, and make the most of the time for a quick recharge—both of the car's batteries and your own. That way you will arrive at your destination feeling totally relaxed.

For us, the concept of "slow travel" doesn't mean literally driving slowly, but rather leaving the hectic pace and stress of everyday life

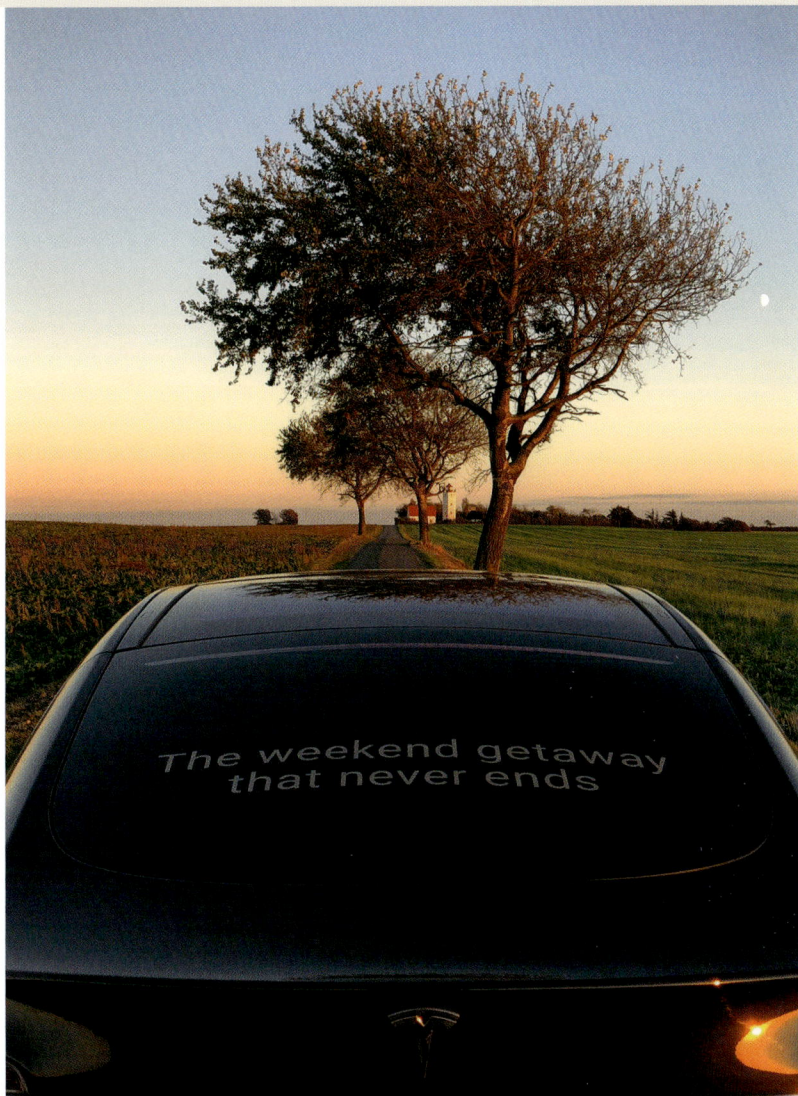

↑ Our way to a more sustainable future.

behind. There will undoubtedly be people who prefer to race up the highway for eight to twelve hours at a time with minimal stops; but although that would be no problem with a fully electric car, everything else literally gets left by the wayside.

So be sure to remember one thing: Enjoy the journey!

We wish you happy travels!

THANKS AND OUTLOOK

Our car was the starting point on our way to a more sustainable future. Elon Musk, Franz von Holzhausen, and Tesla's mission to accelerate the world's transition to sustainable energy have inspired us. What began with the purchase of our Tesla Model S, evolved into an entirely new lifestyle.

We would like to thank all Tesla employees and enthusiasts, and in particular the Tesla Owners Clubs all over the world. On our long journey, they ensured that we never had to travel alone, but found a family ready and waiting in every country. We have always been welcomed by Tesla owners and at Tesla club events. Many people provided us with energy and encouragement along the way. At the same time we not only learned a lot about electromobility, sustainability, and freedom, but we also found out what it means to be together 24/7 on our e-road trip.

A very big thank you goes to our partner myclimate (www.myclimate.org), a non-profit organization based in Switzerland. myclimate offers solutions for effective climate protection—both locally and globally. Together with partners from industry and individuals like ourselves, myclimate aims to help shape the future of the world through consultancy, education, and climate protection projects. Additionally, with their interactive and action-oriented education programs, myclimate encourages everyone to make a contribution to the future. Thanks to our partnership with myclimate, we were able to compensate for our trip's entire carbon footprint.

In Europe alone, we have stayed at 125 different hotels and have come to know and appreciate many different forms of hospitality. Many of them quickly made us feel at home, and ensured that we could recharge our batteries sustainably. A selection of 50 of these hotels are featured in this book. Other excellent destinations can be found on our website, www.MrandMrsTonTour.com. Become a part of our mission! After all, you, too, can easily make your next journey more sustainable—thanks to electromobility, companies such as myclimate, and businesses to whom sustainability means more than just striving for a positive external perception.

Outlook

Taking the decision to leave our apartment, our jobs, our friends and family, and our own comfort zone was certainly not easy. But after our Tesla Model S had taken us safely through 14 European countries and to wonderful destinations on many fantastic routes, we wanted to go further—once around the world. Thanks to Tesla owners, who provided us with their own cars for local travel, we are discovering many more destinations around the globe: New Zealand, Australia, Canada, and the United States are all on the agenda. We'll be back in Europe by the end of 2019, but who knows where the journey will take us next—true to the motto "the weekend getaway that never ends ... ."

To be continued!

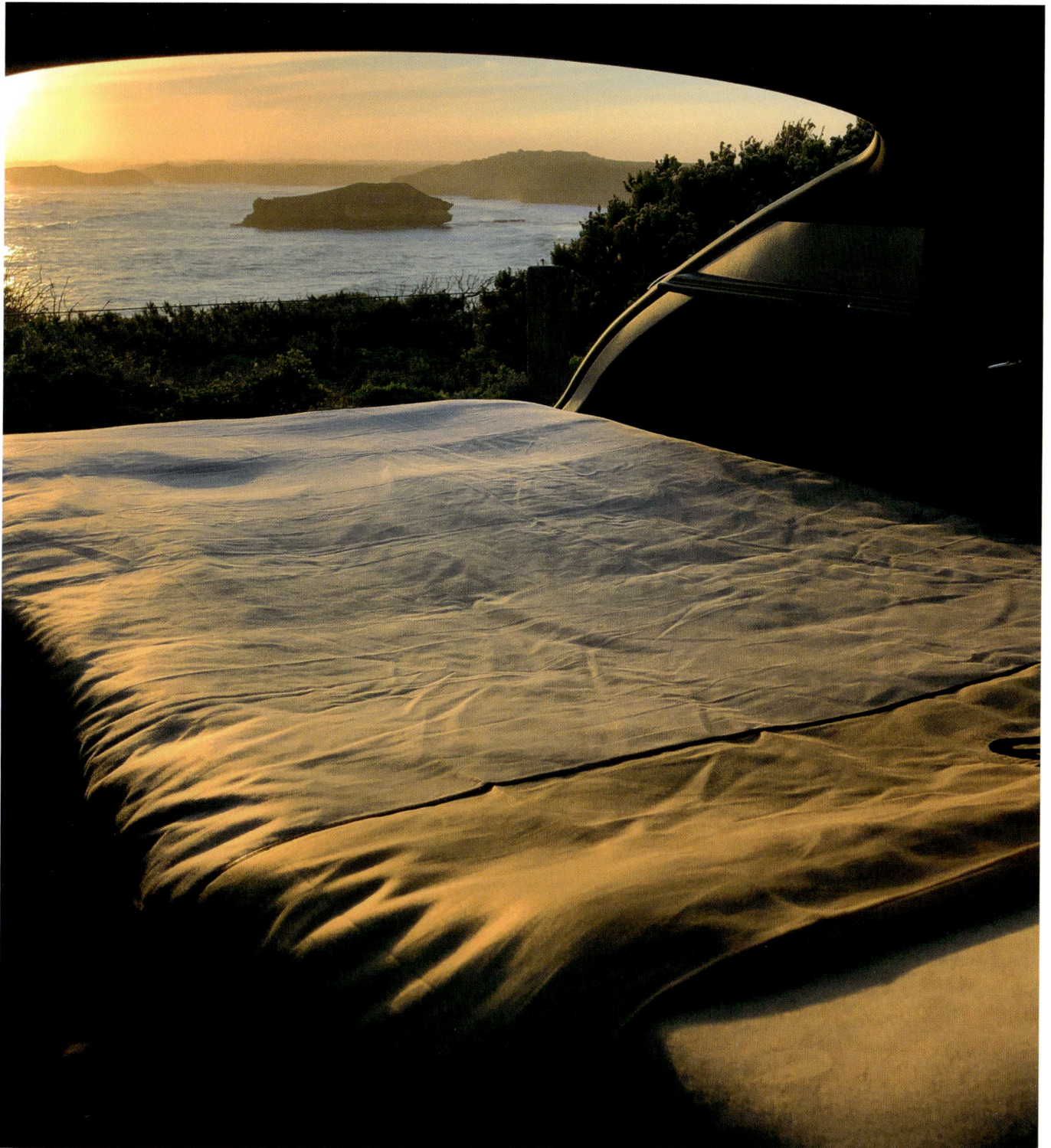

↑ The journey of Mr & Mrs T on Tour continues. Here we are enjoying the sunset in Australia. With a dreamcase on board, the Tesla Model S transformes into the most flexible "hotel" of our entire journey. www.dreamcase.eu

DECLARATION, ABBREVIATIONS, SOURCES

DECLARATION
The authors are not commissioned or hired by Tesla Inc., nor were they sponsored in any way by Tesla. The entire contents of this book reflects solely their personal opinion, and not the views of Tesla or any of its subsidiaries.

ABBREVIATIONS WE USED TO INDICATE THE LOCAL CHARGING FACILITIES
DeC = Destination Charger
SuC = Supercharger
Unless otherwise stated, these use Type 2 connectors.
all EVs = All suitably equipped electric vehicles.

SOURCES FOR THE INFORMATION ON PP. 212–213
Federal Ministry for Environment, Nature Conservation and Nuclear Safety (Germany): informational videos on the Ministry's homepage, retrieved on November 14, 2019, under:
www.bmu.de/media/mobiler-wandel-warum-e-mobilitaet/
www.bmu.de/media/mobiler-wandel-erneuerbare-energien/
www.bmu.de/media/mobiler-wandel-lebensqualitaet/
www.bmu.de/media/mobiler-wandel-rohstoffe/
(information in German)

CREDITS

Cover: image from David Mark at Pixabay

ADLER Spa Resort THERMAE: pp. 72 (salcher thaddaeus), 74 (NICOLA TANZELLA PHOTOGRAPHY), 75b; **Adobe Stock:** pp. 23 (Simon Dannhauer), 47b (Iakov Filimonov), 56 (stevanzz), 83b (DavidArts), 87t (MILAN CHUDOBA), 113t (PCW), 131 (MICHAEL JAEGER), 137b (Oleksandr Prykhodko), 138 (Jan Christopher Becke), 149 (iralex), 167b (Pixelheld), 167t (orpheus26), 169 (Michael Erhardsson), 179b (pelillos), 203 (Wolf Wieland), 204 (Berty), 205 (Manuel Schönfeld), 208 (Christoph Stoeckl); **Barefoot Hotel:** pp. 122 (Nikolaj Georgiew), 123 (Nikolaj Georgiew), 124 (Nikolaj Georgiew), 129 (both, Nikolaj Georgiew); **Fattoria San Martino:** p. 81; **Domaine de la Tortinière:** p. 50; **Getty Images/iStockphoto:** pp. 13 (Cezary Wojtkowski), 19t (TasfotoNL), 21 (Sergey_Peterman), 22 (ribeiroantonio), 31 (SeanPavonePhoto), 37t (XabiTovar), 47t (GeirSteneLarsen), 53t (KenWiedemann), 67 (Julia700702), 77t (mrohana), 83t (Ekaterina Loginova), 87b (robertonencini), 91 (dp3010), 105b (Hermsdorf), 105t (tanukiphoto), 109 (teptong), 117t (Bumblee_Dee), 130 (venemama), 151 (bukki88), 161 (tupungato), 191b (irisphoto2), 201t (undefined undefined), 201b (argalis); all maps: Austria (rbiedermann), Belgium (rbiedermann), Denmark (rbiedermann), France (rbiedermann), Germany (rbiedermann), Liechtenstein (Thitima Thongkham), Norway (kosmozoo), Portugal (rbiedermann), Spain (egoworks), Sweden (IIerlok_Xolms), Switzerland (rbiedermann), The Netherlands (rbiedermann); **Heurigenhof Bründlmayer:** pp. 182, 183, 184 (both); **Hotel Auersperg:** pp. 186 (FOTO FLAUSEN – Andreas Brandl), 187 (FOTO FLAUSEN – Andreas Brandl), 188, 189b (FOTO FLAUSEN – Andreas Brandl), 189t; **Hotel Limmathof:** pp. 110 (all); **Hotel Maria Cristina:** p. 35t; **Hotel Nivå 84:** p. 159; **Hotel Öschberghof:** pp. 144, 145, 146, 147 (both); **Hotel Schwarzer Adler Franz Keller:** p. 142b (Lucie Greiner); **Hotel sevenoaks:** pp. 128 (Brigitte Wegner), 129 (Irene Wernsing); **Hotel Vienna House Andel's Berlin:** pp. 132, 134 (Vienna House); **il Paluffo Tuscan Villa:** p. 85; **MOHR life resort:** pp. 192, 194, 196 (Thorben Jureczko), 197b (Thorben Jureczko); **Mr & Mrs T on Tour:** pp. 6 (both), 7 (both), 8, 10, 11, 12 (both), 15, 16, 17b, 20, 24, 26, 27, 28, 29, 30, 32, 33, 34, 35b, 37b, 38, 40, 41, 42, 44, 45, 48, 51, 53b, 54, 55, 58, 59, 60, 62, 63, 64, 65, 66 (both), 68, 70, 73, 75t, 77b, 78, 79, 80, 84, 88, 90, 92, 93, 94, 95, 96, 97, 98, 99, 101, 106, 108, 111, 118, 120, 121, 133, 135 (both), 140, 141, 142t, 143, 150 (both), 152, 154, 155, 156, 157, 158, 160, 168 (both), 170, 171, 172, 174, 175, 176 (both), 177, 179t, 180, 193, 195 (all), 197t, 200, 201, 202 (both), 206, 209, 211, 212, 214, 219, 221; **Naturhotel Rainer:** pp. 100 (both), 102, 103 (both); **Park Hotel Sonnenhof:** pp. 114 (both), 115; **Pena Park Hotel:** pp. 14, 17t; **shutterstock:** pp. 19b, 39 (dmitro2009), 113b (Oscity), 117b (footageclips), 127t (Mapics), 127b (LaMiaFotografia), 137t (Diego Gorzalczany), 185 (Leonid Andronov), 191t (Boat Rungchamrussopa), 207 (yakub88); **VDD Valeriano Di Domenico:** p. 5; **Yasuragi:** pp. 162, 163, 164 (both), 165

IMPRINT

Mr & Mrs T on Tour
Ralf Schwesinger & Nicole Wanner
e-mail: hello@mrandmrstontour.com
Web: www.mrandmrstontour.com

Texts: Holger Hühn, Augsburg, Ralf Schwesinger, Baden (CH),
Nicole Wanner, Baden (CH)
Translations: Sylvia Goulding, Emily Plank (English)
Copyediting: Lesley Robb
Proofreading: Mike Goulding
Coordination of the English edition: bookwise GmbH, München
Design by Robin John Berwing, teNeues Media
Image editing: Lana Repro, Lana, Italy
Editorial coordination by Inga Wortmann-Grützmacher,
teNeues Media
Production by Nele Jansen, teNeues Media

English edition: ISBN 978-3-96171-232-8
Library of Congress Number: 2019945218

Printed in Slovakia

Bibliographic information published by the Deutsche
Nationalbibliothek

The Deutsche Nationalbibliothek lists this publication in the Deutsche
Nationalbibliografie; detailed bibliographic data are available on the
Internet at http://dnb.dnb.de.

teNeues Publishing Group
Kempen
Berlin
London
Munich
New York
Paris

teNeues

Published by teNeues Publishing Group

teNeues Media GmbH & Co. KG
Am Selder 37, 47906 Kempen, Germany
Phone: +49-(0)2152-916-0
Fax: +49-(0)2152-916-111
e-mail: books@teneues.com

Press department: Andrea Rehn
Phone: +49-(0)2152-916-202
e-mail: arehn@teneues.com

teNeues Media GmbH & Co. KG
Munich Office
Pilotystraße 4, 80538 Munich, Germany
Phone: +49-(0)89-9042-13-200
e-mail: bkellner@teneues.com

teNeues Media GmbH & Co. KG
Berlin Office
Mommsenstraße 43, 10629 Berlin, Germany
Phone: +49-(0)152-0851-1064
e-mail: ajasper@teneues.com

teNeues Publishing Company
350 7th Avenue, Suite 301, New York, NY 10001, USA
Phone: +1-212-627-9090
Fax: +1-212-627-9511

teNeues Publishing UK Ltd.
12 Ferndene Road, London SE24 0AQ, UK
Phone: +44-(0)20-3542-8997

teNeues France S.A.R.L.
39, rue des Billets, 18250 Henrichemont, France
Phone: +33-(0)2-4826-9348
Fax: +33-(0)1-7072-3482

www.teneues.com

FSC
www.fsc.org

MIX
Aus verantwortungs-
vollen Quellen
FSC® C023577